Explorations in World Ethnology

ROBERT B. EDGERTON and L. L. LANGNESS
University of California, Los Angeles

General Editors

Tetum Ghosts and Kin

FIELDWORK IN AN INDONESIAN COMMUNITY

David Hicks

🌳 *Mayfield Publishing Company*

Library of Congress Catalog Card Number: 76-28114
International Standard Book Number: 0-87484-368-5

Manufactured in the United States of America
Mayfield Publishing Company
285 Hamilton Avenue, Palo Alto, California 94301

Sponsoring editor was Alden C. Paine, Carole Norton
supervised editing, and Gene Tanke was manuscript editor.
Michelle Hogan supervised production, and the text and
cover were designed by Nancy Sears. Maxine J. Hicks,
the author's wife, was photographer.

Contents

Acknowledgements

Besides those Caraubalo villagers mentioned in the following chapters, I wish to thank those villagers whose names do not appear but without whose help my field research would have been impossible, and the following individuals and institutions for their assistance: the late Professor Sir Edward Evan Evans-Pritchard, Professor Christoph von Fürer-Haimendorf, Dr. Ravi Jain, Professor H. G. Schulte Nordholt, Dr. Barbara Ward, Mr. Ruy Cinatti, Dr. José Teles, Mr. John Burton, the Junta de Investigações do Ultramar, and the Frederick Soddy Trust. My fieldwork was made possible by a grant from the London Committee of the London-Cornell Project for East and Southeast Asian Studies which was supported jointly by the Carnegie Corporation of New York and the Nuffield Foundation. Before leaving for Indonesia I had the advantage of studying social anthropology at Oxford University in the scholarly havens provided by St. Edmund Hall in my first year and Exeter College in subsequent years. To the Principal and Fellows of St. Edmund Hall, and to the Rector and Fellows of Exeter College go my profound thanks. I am especially grateful for the honor the Rector and Exeter Fellows bestowed on me by my election to the Alan Coltart Scholarship in Anthropology in 1963–1964 and again in 1964–1965. Much of the material examined in this book was analyzed while I was a doctorate student at Oxford working under the supervision of Dr. Rodney Needham. My personal and scholarly debt to him is incalculable. Dr. Melody Trott, of California

State College, commented on an earlier version of the present text, as did Drs. Robert Edgerton and Lew Langness of the University of California, and my colleague at the State University of New York at Stony Brook, Dr. W. Arens. With extraordinarily painstaking care Mr. Gene Tanke went over my entire manuscript and helped improve it in many ways. Mrs. Mari Walker typed and retyped various drafts in her usual patient manner, and I thank her yet again. Many of my descriptions of Tetum life were first presented to my own freshmen and graduate students at Stony Brook, and their reactions helped shape the account given here. I completed this book while a Fellow of the École Pratique des Hautes Études (University of Paris) in 1976, and I wish to thank the SSRC Fellowship Panel in the U.K. and the EPHE in Paris for providing me with the opportunity to exchange ethnographic information and discuss the interpretation of data with those of my French colleagues who have also carried out fieldwork on Timor—Drs. Brigitte Clamagirand, Claudine Berthe, and Gérard Francillon. Their contributions to the seminar series I gave from February to May helped me to regard my Tetum data from alternative points of view, and it was an agreeable experience working with them. Drs. Pierre Smith and Dan Sperber provided me with sounding boards for certain of my ideas, and they, too, merit my thanks. It gives me special pleasure to remark on the encouragement Gabor Nadasty, Marietta Nadasty, Phyllis Newman, Jack and Nancy Garraway, and my mother, Anastasia Dorothy Hicks, have given me at different times while I was writing this book; and as an affectionate token of appreciation for the help she has selflessly given—and continues to give—I dedicate it to my wife, Maxine.

École Pratique des Hautes Études,
University of Paris,
April 1976

Editors' preface

Anthropology, like all scientific and artistic disciplines, is constantly changing so that research approaches once generally favored inevitably give way to new approaches over time. One of the most important developments in contemporary cultural anthropology is the attempt to analyze cultural phenomena in terms of their symbolic significance instead of, or in addition to, their structural, functional, and ecological significance. This approach has given rise to a new sub-discipline that is often referred to as symbolic anthropology. Because symbolic anthropology is such a new development its practitioners vary considerably in the ways they structure their studies; and because the symbolic is abstract in its nature, its impact is often difficult to measure, analyze, and describe in concrete terms. For these reasons, there has so far been little published in the way of useful text materials for students who might wish to pursue their own studies in the field. We believe this account by David Hicks will help to rectify that situation.

Religion, of course, is the primary arena for symbolic meanings and acts. Therefore it is not at all surprising that the advent of symbolic anthropology has been accompanied by a resurgence of interest in the study of non-Western, non-literate religions. This revival has been particularly marked in British social anthropology, of which Professor Hicks is a representative. By concentrating on ghosts and kin in this analysis of the symbols employed in the ritual and myth of the Tetum society,

Professor Hicks enables us to understand much of how the world view of the society relates to its religion. As he himself observes: "When we examine Tetum culture, taking the ritual relationship between ancestral ghosts and their human kin as our starting point, such different spheres as rituals, religious beliefs, kinship practices, oral literature, ecology, and architecture together blend into a single, expansive field of study." Thus the book is not only a useful example of symbolic analysis, but it also demonstrates the functional integration of culture which has fascinated anthropologists for at least the past half century.

David Hicks was trained in social anthropology at the University of Oxford under the late Professor E. E. Evans-Pritchard and Professor Rodney Needham. After winning a scholarship in anthropology at Oxford he went to Indonesia to carry out fieldwork. With the material he collected there, he wrote one thesis that gained him his Doctor of Philosophy degree from Oxford and another that earned him a Doctor of Philosophy degree from the University of London. The author of two dozen or so essays in anthropology, Dr. Hicks here presents his first book.

Robert B. Edgerton

L. L. Langness

Tetum Ghosts and Kin

Fieldwork

1

The malevolent soul was invisible. But the people who call themselves the Tetum could sense its presence. Stretching out my hand to steady the coffin housing the remains of the well-known elder, Cai Tuli, I suddenly felt the restraining hand of old Leal Soares. Another elder, Leal was a cautious man of seventy. Both came from the village of Mane Hat ("the community of the four brothers"). That clammy afternoon on the equatorial isle of Timor, in Indonesia, the coffin bearers were heaving their burden around so recklessly I feared the corpse might be tossed out. Keeping my hold, I glanced sideways at him as he warned, "The soul of the dead man is trying to re-enter the corpse. Stay clear! There's danger here for you!" Was he feigning concern to stop me seeing the finale of this fascinating ritual of death?

"If all the soul wants is to return to the corpse, why should it bother me? I don't wish to prevent it," I replied.

"Maybe. But that doesn't count. The boys carrying the coffin are too strong. Soon it will be mad with anger," he explained. "Take my advice, and stand back! We Tetum know what we are doing. The dead soul will vent its spite on someone ignorant of its tricks."

For the sake of peace I let the exchange end there. Leal led me to a safer place. Leaving the encircling forest, the funeral cortège hastened into the cemetery.

My chief purpose in this book is to show how ritual in a nonliterate community brings together many different facets of that community's culture—religious beliefs, kinship practices, literature, ecology, even the architecture of the house—and unites them in a comprehensive system. The community in this case is the population of the two villages of Mamulak and Mane Hat, which together make up the aristocratic half of a princedom known as Caraubalo. This princedom is found in one of the three main regions inhabited by the Tetum people of eastern Indonesia, among whom I lived and worked for fifteen months. Certain details of culture in Mamulak differ from those in Mane Hat, and I shall point these out when necessary. Otherwise, when making observations common to both villages I shall use the names Mamulak and Mane Hat interchangeably.

To put this first chapter in its proper context, here is a sketch of the book as a whole. I begin by discussing the circumstances of my fieldwork and outlining the more basic aspects of Tetum life (chapter 1). Then I consider the beliefs which provide Tetum religion with its ideology, and describe the rite which opens the Tetum cycle of existence. This is the birth ritual (chapter 2). In chapter 3 I examine the connection between ritual and ecology, and we follow one family's activities around the seasonal calendar. The location for many rituals is the Tetum house, and chapter 4 describes its symbolic structure. Chapter 5 traces the web of kinship relations that surrounds each family. The ritual expression of kinship and marriage occupy our attention in chapter 6, and the cycle of Tetum existence ends in the final chapter (7) with an account of the death ritual.

Before learning something of Eastern Timor and the ways in which I obtained information from its inhabitants, we should consider for a moment fieldwork in general.

Fieldwork is a part of every anthropologist's education, and although research in rural and urban communities in the United States constitutes "fieldwork" in its broadest sense, scholars who have worked among non-literate peoples in conditions far removed from Western experience have always emphasized the benefits that can be gained from studying societies whose customs contrast most vividly with our own. In fact, some anthropologists distinguish between cultural anthropology and sociology by arguing that anthropology is concerned with the study of non-literate peoples whereas sociology studies "ourselves."

Over the years, as hypotheses and theories are formulated and forgotten, field research will continue to add to our knowledge of how non-literate contemporary peoples live, and the data collected will endure long after the cultures we describe have become extinct. The desire to record information that will soon be unrecordable encourages many a fieldworker to endure unusual hardships patiently. I went to Timor to learn about a culture that was on the point of being overtaken by Westernization.

Intensive fieldwork by an anthropologist who involves himself in the lives of the people he is studying began early this century with Franz Boas of the United States and Bronislaw Malinowski of England. The practice until then had been for armchair scholars to sift through masses of written information on such non-literate peoples as the Australian aborigines, Eskimos, and Bantu, hunting out facts to support theories they had thought up beforehand. They wanted to trace the evolution of Western society by placing the institutions and beliefs of non-literate peoples (which they had discovered by reading the journals and reports of missionaries, administrators, and travelers) at what they imagined to be appropriate steps on a hypothetical evolutionary scale. These early students of non-literate cultures equated "primitive" or "non-literate" with "primeval," and believed that non-literate peoples existing at that time corresponded to prehistoric man. At the bottom of the scale they would place that institution or belief they thought the most primitive, then just above it they would insert the next most primitive specimen, and so on, until at the top they would place the customs of the Victorian Age. These they believed to be the acme of social evolution. The most celebrated of these scholars, Sir James Frazer (1854–1901), in his well-known book *The Golden Bough*, ranked magic below religion and religion below science in his schema of Western man's intellectual development. But when asked if he had actually seen one of the non-literates he wrote so confidently about he was reported to have replied, aghast, "God forbid!"

By the 1920's, however, fieldwork was an established technique in anthropological scholarship, and as the decades have passed the tools of investigation have improved, so that we now have an ever-expanding mass of exact information on non-literate peoples.

Let us now briefly consider the background to my fieldwork.

EASTERN TIMOR

For five hundred years the emerald and brown islands which straddle the Equator to form the East Indies were dominated by three rival powers—Great Britain, The Netherlands, and Portugal. Then came the Second World War, which shattered European hegemony in the region and led to the birth of Indonesia and Malayasia as independent states.

3

Until 1975 a tiny piece of the archipelago still retained colonial links with Europe. This was Portuguese Timor, governed by a nation whose sailors, traders, and missionaries were the first Europeans to gaze upon its sandy beaches, precipitous sea-cliffs, and swampy lagoons.

No one knows exactly when Timor was first sighted from a Portuguese ship. We hear it first mentioned in a letter dated January 6, 1514, written by Rui de Brito, so probably this sighting occurred sometime between 1500 and 1514. Timor's drawing power lay in the forests of sandalwood which grew bountifully in many places, and as the decades passed an increasing number of Portuguese, and later, Dutchmen, found themselves attracted to this wealth. These earlier adventurers described an isle covered with a patchwork of warring kingdoms, a country in which military alliances dominated inter-kingdom politics. The sixteenth century saw two rival native empires, the Belu and the Servião, controlling the destinies of these kingdoms. The Belu ruled eastern Timor and some of western Timor; the Servião governed the region now inhabited by the Atoni. Wars between the Portuguese and Dutch eventually destroyed both empires.

At least fourteen linguistic groups occur on the island, and all belong to the Malayo-Polynesian language family. (See Figure 2.) Tetum belongs to the Indonesian language branch of that family. The Tetum people (variously called the Tetu, Tetun, Fehan, or Belu), who total about 150,000, are conveniently divided into three groups: the Northern Tetum, the Southern Tetum and the Eastern Tetum. The Northern and Southern groups are collectively known as the Western Tetum. Viqueque district falls within the Eastern Tetum zone.

At the time of my fieldwork in 1966 and 1967 Portuguese Timor consisted of a small western enclave and the whole eastern half of the island of Timor, the largest of the Lesser Sunda group in the extreme eastern section of the East Indies. The western half was Indonesian territory. In December 1975, after months of intrigue in the east, the Indonesian army crossed the frontier and invaded its little neighbor. It quickly imposed its will upon the people, who with the departure of the Portuguese now find themselves under the control of another colonial power. The administrative system I observed will not last much longer, although the indigenous system of princedoms, villages, and hamlets will endure for another generation or so.

Eastern Timor in 1966 was governed through ten districts, each ruled by an Administrator. A district was split into various posts, each ruled by a chief of post and made up of princedoms. Every princedom was administered by a chief responsible for supervising those villages fall-

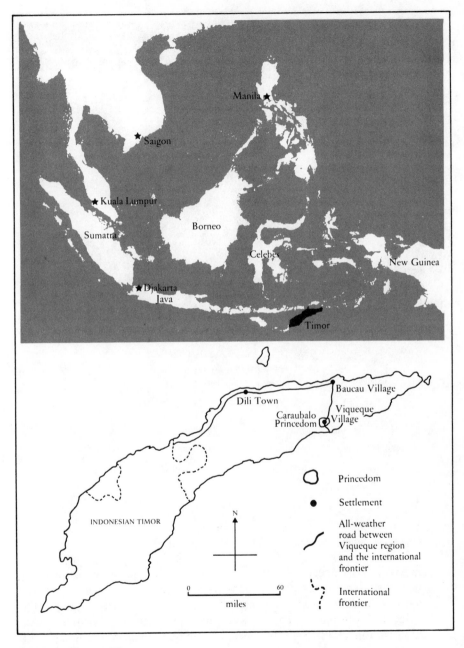

Figure 1   Eastern Timor

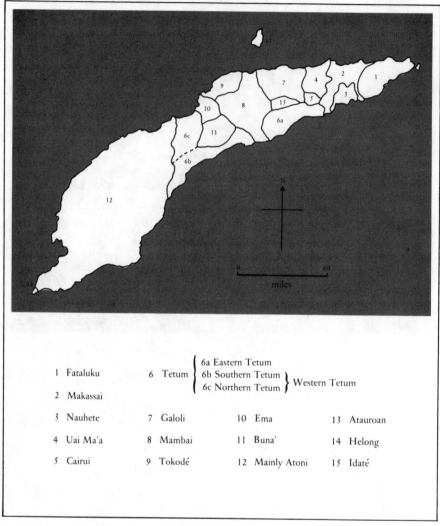

Figure 2   Linguistic regions of Timor

1 Fataluku	6 Tetum	6a Eastern Tetum		
		6b Southern Tetum	} Western Tetum	
2 Makassai		6c Northern Tetum		
3 Nauhete	7 Galoli	10 Ema	13 Atauroan	
4 Uai Ma'a	8 Mambai	11 Buna'	14 Helong	
5 Cairui	9 Tokodé	12 Mainly Atoni	15 Idaté	

ing within his princedom. A headman ruled the village, which is a dispersed settlement comprising many hamlets, each containing up to about a dozen houses. Hamlets are separated from one another by jungle. The chief, and to some degree, the headman, represented the Portuguese Administration, and though they were elected by the villagers, their appointment had to be ratified by Administration officials before they could assume office. This bureaucratic system and settlement pattern was common to all eastern Timor. At the summit of the administrative hierarchy was the Governor, who, until the political coup of August 10, 1975, mediated between this overseas province and the government in Lisbon. His seat was the provincial capital of Dili, which is located on the north coast and has a population of about 10,000 Europeans, Timorese, Chinese, and Arabs. It is far larger than any other settlement in eastern Timor. Baucau, the site of the only international airport, with a mere 1,000 residents, is the second largest settlement. Both, together with Viqueque Village, are geographically located in Figure 1.

In the Portuguese language the chief of a princedom is called the *chefe de suku,* though the indigenous title *liurai* is occasionally heard on the island. This title was formerly applied only to kings who ruled

The Uma Kik princedom chief, Miguel Soares, in ceremonial garb. Before Europeans imposed a firm colonial hand on Timor such chiefs would lead their warriors into head-hunting forays outfitted like this. In Miguel Soares' hand is a war-sword, on his head a golden buffalo-horn ornament and on his chest a golden disc. His wristwatch is material evidence of acculturation!

territories known as *rai* ("kingdoms"). Dozens of kingdoms, each made up of princedoms, covered the island in mosaic fashion. Sometime before the Second World War the Portuguese broke up these kingdoms into their constituent princedoms, reorganizing the princedoms into posts. The office of king vanished, and the term *liurai* came to be applied to the chiefs, whose office was another innovation. Before the creation of chiefs, two native officials, the *macair fukun* (whose office belonged to Mane Hat village) and the *dato ua'in* (whose office belonged to Mamulak), jointly governed the princedom "as the husband and wife rule the household, loving their dependents and respecting each other." Since both were also headmen of their respective villages I shall translate their respective titles as "Mane Hat headman" and "Mamulak headman." Their offices persist. But their authority has passed to the chief. This dual authority in traditional government is common in Indonesian political systems; Professor H. G. Schulte Nordholt (1971) has described how it works for the Atoni peoples of Western Timor.

Before I left for the East Indies a friend of mine in the Portuguese civil service had advised me to choose the Viqueque area for fieldwork. It was, he thought, an area where the least westernized Timorese lived, and where the type of kinship system I was interested in still operated. Viqueque district has five posts. The post that concerns us is called the "Home Post." From it the Viqueque Administrator governs the ten princedoms of his district. The administrative buildings are in Caraubalo princedom. Although this princedom has seven native villages, the Administration had built its own special settlement, Viqueque Village, which contains the Administrator's house, the Administration buildings, a school, an infirmary, about half a dozen Chinese shops, and an assortment of other buildings which in their different ways cater to the Europeans and Chinese. Those few Timorese who live here work in the Administration or are employed by non-bureaucratic Europeans or Chinese. My wife and I lived here, in an abandoned Chinese shop. From there we visited the local hamlets each day.

FIRST DAYS ON THE ISLAND

Timor had aroused my interest because of the close relationship, reported by missionaries, between kinship and religion in the societies found on the island. To acquire more knowledge of Timor and obtain official support for my visa application, I stayed in Lisbon from January to April of 1965. In December my wife and I received visas to go, and in that month, too, our son Paul was born. When we left England on the afternoon of February 2, 1966, he was still only a few weeks old.

My chief worries at that time were two problems every fieldworker must solve: language and residence. I had found no opportunity to learn spoken Tetum, and had nightmares about returning to my university with empty notebooks. The difficulty with residence was simply that no one had actually invited me. I was going to work in a community as a total stranger. Even the name and place of "my" community were unknown to me. My mind kept returning to the question of where to sleep the first night, and what reception to expect once I had decided upon a village. I had visions of sleeping in some snake-infested jungle, or worse, trying to snatch some sleep in a rat-infested cornfield after having been refused entry to my chosen community.

We dallied en route, arriving at the Baucau airport on Wednesday, March 9. Although I did not know it then, another three months would pass before we settled in Viqueque. After taking three days to recuperate from the long journey, we traveled the 130 kilometers from Baucau to Dili by jeep to introduce ourselves to the Governor. The trip should have taken five and a half hours. Instead, because the vehicle broke down twice, had a flat tire, and the driver found the River Manatuto (the biggest barrier between the two settlements) difficult to ford, we took eight hours. Our arrival was at 5:30 P.M. In Dili we learned that the only house available in Viqueque Village was a rundown Chinese shop, the property of a Dili-based trading company. We got permission to rent it and were told the company architect would visit Viqueque the following week to determine how much work would be necessary to make the building inhabitable. Secure in this promise we returned on March 30 to the delightful inn at Baucau and our attentive hostess, Miss Maria da Figueira. On his way to Viqueque, the architect passed through Baucau on April 2, and spent the night at the inn. When he asked if we wanted to see our future home, our response was automatic. But when I set eyes on the shop, 67 kilometers away in Viqueque, it was so obviously in need of repair I spent the two-hours return ride in misery.

It seemed the forthcoming weeks would be wasted, but as things turned out the future was not all that dismal. I was able to carry out fieldwork among the Makassai communities scattered around the Baucau inn, and later we were able to travel around the far eastern part of the island thanks to an obliging Portuguese lieutenant who drove us there in his jeep. Also, by staying in Baucau we established a base from which to obtain medical supplies, baby foods, rolls of film, clothing, and other items unavailable in Viqueque. Maria da Figueira and other Baucau friends could help us acquire even scarcer items from Australia, and we knew if our daily lives in the field proved trying we could recuperate in Baucau with amiable people in restful surroundings. Anything unobtainable in Timor could be flown from Australia to Baucau. Our friends there would take care of such matters as customs, formalities, and transportation to Viqueque.

We arrived at our house in Viqueque on Thursday, June 2, before the repairs were completed. Once installed, I discovered several things: that Viqueque Village was the geographical center of both Caraubalo princedom and the Home Post, which contained another nine princedoms; that while a slight majority of the post's residents spoke Tetum, almost as many spoke the Makassai language and another called Cairui; that almost all Tetum were Christian, whereas those who spoke the other languages were all pagan; and that each princedom chief owned one house in his princedom and one in Viqueque Village itself, so as to be at hand when the Administrator wanted him. The Secretary of the district kindly gave me a map of the post and a list of its fifty-two villages (grouped into the ten princedoms), and when I later sought the advice of the late Miguel da Costa Soares, the well-informed chief of Uma Ua'in Craik princedom (one of the ten), he was able to tell me whether a village was Tetum or non-Tetum, Christian or pagan. I wanted a Tetum village that was predominately pagan. These were few, he said, but one or two did exist—in the most distant Tetum princedom, Bibileu. Eight hours' journey on horseback into hills also inhabited by Makassai and Cairui, it seemed isolated enough to have protected its ancient customs. Armed with this information I asked the Administrator, perhaps the most efficient on the island, if he could arrange a house for me in Bibileu. On August 12 he told me I now had one in a village called Háre Oan, adding that ten days later the annual census of the entire Home Post was due to begin with a survey of this particular princedom. The census is made by about four officials who travel from princedom to princedom on horseback, and he offered me a ride.

A census team spends as much time in each of the ten princedoms as is necessary to complete its survey. The questionnaire for each villager in the princedom is completed at the chief's princedom residence. Depending upon the size of the population, this work may take as few as three, or as many as fifteen, hours. A princedom remote from Viqueque Village and with a large population may keep a team busy at the chief's residence for two days and a night. Bibileu is the Home Post's fourth largest princedom, so my companions spent the night of August 22 there. I helped in their secretarial work, adding my own novel queries as each

Timorese man walked up to our table: "What is your religion? What language do you speak?" Religion was my criterion of acculturation, and by the time the horses were mounted to take the team to the next princedom, which happened to be Uai Mori, I had learned that the Bibileu Tetum were far more Christianized than I had been told. So I decided to find out for myself just what the relationship between religion and language in the whole of the Home Post really was. I asked the Secretary if I might accompany the team to Uai Mori. He readily agreed. With intermittent visits to Viqueque Village to relax with Maxine and Paul, I spent the following two weeks collecting information from all the Home Post princedoms. When I had returned home after the final excursion, I decided that before going to Háre Oan I would spend a couple of days sifting through my data to assure myself that that far-off village really suited my needs best.

Very soon I perceived Miguel da Costa Soares had not been entirely accurate. Most of what he had said was sound, but he was unaware that of the five predominately Tetum princedoms in the Home Post (Caraubalo, Uma Ua'in Craik, Balarauain, Uma Kik, and Bibileu), it was not the last which was the most pagan, but the first. That princedom coming closest to my ideal was the one I already lived in! Of its six Tetum villages those of Mamulak and Mane Hat actually had more pagans than Christians.

Pleased as I was, there was the problem of my Bibileu house. I had to ask the Administrator to let the Bibileu chief, José, know my plans had changed. So, a little abashed, I requested another house, this time in either Mane Hat or Mamulak. Again the Administrator consented. I left his house satisfied I would soon be a resident of one of these two villages. As it happened, the house was never built. Communications between the Caraubalo chief and the Administrator may have broken down somewhere. Or perhaps the Administrator feared I might change my mind a second time. All my fieldwork was therefore carried out from our Viqueque Village house; my wife and I walking each day from Viqueque Village to the Caraubalo hamlets we were interested in, to spend the morning or the afternoon, and sometimes the evening.

Fieldworkers trained in the tradition of observer-participation expect to live in the heart of the native community, learning the language and becoming familiar with the customs by immersing themselves in them. I had never thought of doing anything else. For a few weeks I looked upon my daily expeditions from Viqueque Village simply as a way of filling an interim period while my new house was being built. Yet things turned out for the best. Living inside the community would have taught us the Tetum language faster, and we would have been more speedily and thoroughly accepted as participants in village life. In a community whose members were apprehensive about our intentions, it would have been more difficult for them to have kept obscure customs from us. We should have made friends more quickly. Yet there were two advantages to living outside the community. First, we were better able to safeguard our health and that of our baby; the daily regime of hygiene we imposed on our house-boy and house-girl in Viqueque would not have been as feasible in a hamlet. Second, villagers disliked seeing their remarks being taken down in a notebook, and we were obliged to retain whatever information we could in our memories until the end of the day. In Viqueque, at least, I could write up my notes in privacy, and work into the night if I wished. Hamlets have little privacy. To have written there would have invited awkward questions.

AT WORK

In September and October I would leave the house and tramp along the paths linking the hamlets hoping to find someone willing to converse with a stranger whose command of Tetum was worse than that of a four-year-old child. Gardens from the previous year were being burnt off and fences rebuilt. Since few people understandably had the patience to talk to me, I spent hours wandering alone tracing paths and inserting prominent landscape features on maps I was making. If anyone had time to speak, after asking his name and village I would seek the names of any local features for my map. I did not establish any really productive contact until one afternoon, when as I was strolling through a hamlet I later found out was called Cailulik with a Timorese soldier stationed in Viqueque Village, we came upon some people eating a meal. In fluent Tetum my friend asked what was going on. A fourteen-year-old lad jumped to his feet and told him the meal celebrated the final rite of death for a former resident of the hamlet who had been buried exactly a year earlier. I had no idea then what he was talking about. He gave his name as José Pereira and said his home was in the nearby hamlet of Baria Laran. He invited us to eat. During the meal he asked my companion why I had been wandering about the jungle for the last few months. He asked this in Tetum, but I was able to understand what he said, so gave my answer straight to José in Portuguese, explaining my reasons for coming to Timor. José could not take my reply seriously. Why, he was able to ask me many weeks later, should any "civilized" person study the obscure language and "backward" customs of a people whose way of life was "primitive?" José had been educated by Christian missionaries in a high school in Dili, and regarded his newly acquired cultural tastes as superior to his parents' traditions.

Among the educated offspring of chiefs, notably those of Miguel da Costa Soares, I met the same disdain for their culture. They would plead ignorance when asked about traditional religion or kinship institutions, and pictured themselves in the vanguard of a newer society. But though far more westernized than villagers, they were still Timorese. Occupying an intermediate status between the two cultures, they will find it difficult accommodating their mixed Timorese-European heritage to the Indonesian occupation. In 1966 and 1967 they simply could not believe the activities of villagers could hold interest for outsiders. So before long Maxine and I stopped trying to explain our motives.

José was not a chief's son. His parents lived in Mamulak, not Viqueque Village, and as the weeks passed his veneer of contempt for tradition faded. Increasingly, he absented himself from school for lengthy periods, and came to realize that our work had some value. That first afternoon he told us his father, André Pereira (Naha Funok was his Tetum name), would welcome us in his house in the nearby hamlet of Baria Laran. Could we go there tomorrow? He would be happy to call at our house and show us the way. "And don't forget your camera!"

As we were to learn the next day, the forty-two-year old André had received some European education before its course was disrupted by the Japanese invasion of 1942; he had unhappy memories of events during the war years, which he believed prevented him from making a place for himself in the world beyond his village. Still, his few years at school had at least equipped him to converse confidently with members of the Administration. Over the years officials had become accustomed to use André rather than the official headman when they wanted to communicate their policies to the Mamulak residents. Thus André's political influence was increased and his social prestige enhanced. André and his son spoke contemptuously of those of their fellows who were still pagan and illiterate. The headman was one, and because André had been born into a social grouping called Tuna ("The Eel") which did not own this political office, he was permanently ineligible for it. This so irked him he delighted in venting his spleen on the incumbent officeholder and tried to increase his own prestige in the community. André also went out of his way to welcome European visitors. In their presence he could display his sophistication before his impressed companions. Although disparaging about pagans, André contrived to bolster his standing in the community by giving his time generously and presents liberally to other villagers. He was liked and respected by most of them, but was decidedly unpopular with a man called Rubi Loik, a firm upholder of the old religion whom we shall get to know later on.

Next day José led us to his father's house, where André, his wife Hílda, and the rest of the household had gathered to greet us. We talked, ate pork and green vegetables, and drank wine. I had finally started getting data on "my people!" Because my Tetum was still slow we talked in Portuguese. This was the last time I used that language with a villager; from that day on all my conversations, even with André, were in Tetum. As the afternoon lengthened into evening, we took our leave. In our house that night I wrote down what Maxine and I could recall of André's talk on village life. It covered six and a half pages in my notebook. Our only mishap was that the film had not run through the camera. We later discovered that André had increased his social standing by our visit, so it was a fair exchange of benefits. Luckily for me, he had plenty of rivals who did not want to be outshone. Now that André had broken the ice invitations poured in. Our visits to the hamlets multiplied so encouragingly I quickly filled a notebook. Later I switched to a typewriter. This was faster and neater and made copies possible.

Attitudes like those of Miguel's children had infected even village folk, most of whom were burdened with a cultural inferiority complex. The missionaries we knew in Timor had sacrificed years of their lives for the Timorese and were devoted to their welfare, but they were convinced that the native religions were false and certain Timorese customs were immoral. Together with the Portuguese officials they were members of a technologically advanced civilization which sought to change traditional ways of life in the name of "progress." In confronting them it is natural that many Timorese, members of a technologically simple population with no desire to change their ways, should come to regard their own beliefs and practices as backward, and learn to perceive themselves as inferior to outsiders.

Working among such people, the anthropologist may find it difficult getting honest answers to his questions, and may suffer the unwanted attentions of local snobs who see themselves as heralds of a new and progressive order. Several of these, dressed in European fashion and aggressively mouthing their Portuguese, used to crowd around us during our first visits to the hamlets. But when they realized we valued real Tetum customs above pseudo-European ones, they left us alone. When I started talking to someone about a custom missionaries had persuaded him was shameful he would switch the conversation to a less sensitive topic. When I jotted down anything in my notebook my informant would dry up. Maxine and I had to remember scraps of information and write them down privately at home. Tetum words and texts of oral literature villagers allowed us to record openly. They were flattered by our efforts to master their language and keen to make certain we noted down words lest we forgot. Those who cared about their heritage knew the upcoming generation would neglect the ancient narratives, and wanted them made permanent.* Their wariness had been heightened by seeing me cooperate with the census team in their chief's house. In their eyes this association made me a bureaucrat, an inconvenient identification in the early months of my fieldwork, when no one in Mamulak was quite clear what I was up to. The purpose of the census is to get data for taxation, and as villagers suffer lapses of memory when officials ask how many head of livestock they own (the criterion for taxation), they had reason for anxiety when I began what seemed to them an audit. Fieldworkers usually have to face the problem of deciding with which class, caste, or group to identify. Their decision will determine what kind of information they receive and what view of the social world they will become acquainted with. One might try to identify with no single grouping, but in so doing he would risk finishing up alienated from all groups. Initially linked with officials and chiefs, and living in the Administrative village itself, I found it hard to erase this bureaucratic impression. In time, by keeping my contact with officials to a minimum, I was able to erase it.

As this impression weakened, so did our circle of friends widen and my facility in the native language improve. If there is any one path to understanding a foreign community, language is it. Putting a translator between himself and individuals whose habits of thought he seeks to understand clearly hinders the fieldworker. As anyone who speaks a foreign language knows, much is lost in translation. One of the most perceptive of fieldworkers, Edward Evan Evans-Pritchard (1902–1973), once observed that the central problem in fieldwork is translation. To emphasise the importance of this remark a book dedicated to him carried the title *The Translation of Culture*. Evans-Pritchard was talking about translating a *culture*, not just a *language*—an even more difficult task, for the anthropologist's main job is to describe an exotic culture in terms his

*On the journey from England to Timor my tape recorder had been damaged, so all texts had to be written out. Not only would it have made collecting texts vastly more convenient, but a tape recorder would have reduced the need to rely so much on memory. It would also have served another purpose. Whereas villagers disliked my writing down information, they would have enthusiastically welcomed my recording their conversations on tape. Like most of us, the Tetum appreciate the sound of their own voices. To have been mechanically captured in speech would have more than compensated for having information recorded.

readers, who belong to a radically different one, will understand. He can only begin to attempt this if he himself understands the native tongue. Had I not learned Tetum few villagers would have been willing to endure the tedium of a "conversation" with me, and I would have remained as remote from them personally as on the day they first spoke to me—through a Portuguese-speaking interpreter. Fieldwork is a personal commitment. An interpreter intrudes.

At first glance, cultural anthropology's closest ties might seem to be with sociology. After all, both subjects deal with social facts and both profess to understand something called "society." But a crucial difference separates them. Sociologists today study their own society, and however complex (or obscure) their *analyses*, the *contents* of their inquiry form the cultural tradition of their readers, so the problem of translation does not arise. Cultural anthropology has more in common with history, for the historian seeks to *re*present the events, ideas, and customs of a former age in such a way as to make them convey meaning to persons of his own time. It is also closer to literature.

A fieldworker writing his book is in a position similar in some respects to a novelist. His materials have been created for him, but he must present a coherent portrait of what he takes to be the behavior and thought of a community. Yet he cannot transcend his own view of reality. Were several fieldworkers, each holding different theoretical interests and with contrasting personalities, to work in the same community during the same period their books would be quite different. The empirical details of house architecture, death rituals, and ecology might be the same in each account, but even so definitional problems might create difficulties, and perhaps the "facts" themselves stir controversy. To take a Caraubalo example: in recording the total population of a village, fieldworker A might include *all* permanent residents, regardless of where the local bureaucracy considered some individuals to be domiciled. Fieldworker B might accept the official line, and class as inhabitants only those *officially counted* as residents. Mamulak village contains either 375 inhabitants or 350, depending on whether the first or second option is taken. A small matter, perhaps, but suggestive of the impossibility of being "objective" even in an area where at first glance one might suppose "objectivity" unavoidable.

What we should expect from the author of a fieldwork study is not "objectivity" but a dispassionate attempt to present every fact relevant to the standpoint the writer has chosen to adopt, regardless of whether it supports his argument. By "dispassionate" I mean without a compulsion to force data into a pre-selected theoretical framework, to twist evidence

16

or press more claims for the chosen viewpoint than it can support. There is no one angle of approach which alone is valid for a community. My interpretation of Mamulak society, like any anthropologist's interpretation, is not an absolute one. It is more like a photograph taken from one angle. It is a partial view of the whole picture. A similar warning is necessary about the term "social structure." Earlier scholars, notably the English anthropologist A. R. Radcliffe-Brown (1881–1955), used the term to apply to something which was supposed to exist "objectively" at the empirical level. Society was said to resemble in certain particulars a natural organism and its structure supposed to be as "real" as a fish's backbone. Social anthropology was a natural science which classified the different types of social structure. Having done so, it worked out social laws comparable to those in the natural sciences. Instead of discovering laws, however, anthropologists found themselves only classifying and sub-classifying societies. The process was somewhat like butterfly-collecting, and today few anthropologists advocate it. In an empirical sense, of course, a "society" simply does not exist. It is an abstraction. When a scholar finds it useful to talk about "social structure" he is using a mental fabrication, not referring to a thing that exists outside his brain. A community's "social structure," then, is a particular pattern of order chosen for it by an anthropologist because he believes it gives the fullest meaning to the facts he is trying to interpret. What may be a community's "social structure" for one fieldworker may not be so for his colleague. Among the natives themselves, the "social structure" will depend upon the individual's social status and personal experience. A man will regard the social universe in a different way than a woman; an adult in a different way than a child; a political leader in a different way than his followers; a priest in a different way than a layman. Like every fieldworker, I began my inquiries looking for obvious patterns of clear-cut behavior, but soon found life far more disorganized than I would have believed possible from the elegant descriptions of non-literate communities I had read. It took some time for me to appreciate that the order described by these anthropologists was subjective, not "objective," and it became increasingly apparent that Tetum individuals varied in their view of the world.

SETTLING DOWN

Apart from José and André, none of my informants spoke Portuguese, so I was forced to speak Tetum. As one gradually learns to swim without having to touch the bottom every few strokes, so one day I realized I could understand what the villagers were talking about. This happened about April, I think. Maxine had already passed this stage. She has a more retentive linguistic memory and a better faculty for linguistic imitation than I, and could concentrate on the way phrases were put together and words used rather than worrying about what information they contained. I had to sift and evaluate what I heard. Some anthropologists argue that fieldwork should be a solitary undertaking, that spouses are a hindrance. I failed to appreciate the force behind their arguments before I went into the field, and now I sympathize even less. The only serious disadvantage I found to a joint venture is that learning the native language takes longer. After spending the whole day speaking Tetum, Maxine and I could not resist discussing the day's events in English. Thus each morning, upon entering the first hamlet, we would have to restart our minds along their Tetum track. A fieldworker whose only contacts are with native speakers is in a better position to develop linguistic competence quickly. But this is no overwhelming advantage. By the time I left Timor in September 1967 I could verbalize any question that came to mind and understand most of what a villager might say to me when directly addressed. I still had difficulty understanding dialogue between two or more native speakers, partly because they spoke more quickly between themselves and partly because the personal and interpersonal contexts so essential for grasping the nuances in conversations were often left unstated, since speakers knew their listeners already understood these matters. Speaking to us, they realized their speech needed filling out.

In his eagerness to begin fieldwork, an anthropologist may settle himself down in the first interesting community he spies, only to realize later a more attractive population lives elsewhere in the vicinity. The opposite danger lies in searching too long for the "right people"; if he skips from place to place but never settles down anywhere for long, the fieldworker may eventually leave the field with wide-ranging but superficial notes for a large area. Making a brief but careful survey before selecting a community is extremely useful, and I am very glad I helped the 1966 census team record its material.

Birtfi: The cycle opens

2

Leal Soares was right. As the old diplomat had hinted, I understood little of what went on that afternoon in April of 1967. Standing in isolation the individual customs of a people make only limited sense. They need to be viewed as part of a system before they disclose their full meaning. In the field, one of the anthropologist's basic tasks is to find the links which connect particular customs. This accomplished, he can set about establishing the principles which give order to the system thus discovered.

The simplest principles a society can use to order ideas and behavior are "opposition" and "complementarity." Opposition separates; complementarity unites. Both order ideas and behavior more extensively in some societies than in others. Western societies use them much less than many in Indonesia, and the societies on Timor really put them to work. The Tetum who live in Caraubalo arrange some very important ideas into a series of what can be termed *complementary oppositions,* dyads, binary contrasts, or binary pairs.* For convenience they can also be called simply oppositions or contrasts. But we must realize that not only does each term in a binary pair oppose, or contrast with, its opposite; it complements it as well. The most prominent contrasts in Tetum religion and kinship are between human beings *(ema)* and ancestral ghosts *(maté bian)* and between men *(mane)* and women *(feto).*

*Anthropological terms in English that are italicized when they first appear in the text are defined at the back of the book in the List of Anthropological Terms.

SECULAR AND SACRED

Sixty years ago, in his classic book *The Elementary Forms of the Religious Life* (1916), Émile Durkheim (1858–1917) defined religion as "a unified system of beliefs and practices relative to sacred things...which unite into a single moral community, called a church, all those who adhere to them." "Sacred things" were things set apart from things (including persons) that were in the opposite, yet complementary, category of "profane." I prefer the term "secular" to "profane," though both are virtually synonymous. Of this distinction between secular and sacred, which he regarded as basic to religion, Durkheim added (1916:47): "In all the history of human thought there exists no other example of two categories of things so profoundly differentiated or so radically opposed to one another." Even though it is not verbally clothed, the contrast between secular and sacred is as basic to Tetum notions of universal order as it was to this French scholar. The universal order created by a society can be termed a "cosmos," which is an ordered system of ideas. The word itself is related to "cosmetic," a term connected with the idea of order being created. A woman daubs cosmetics on her face to create a new, more attractive order upon the old. A cosmos is a system of order that has already been created.

Mamulak villagers assert that the secular world lies on the earth's surface where humans dwell. Visible and tangible, this region is dominated by men. The sacred world, though inhabited by members of both sexes, is dominated by female ancestral ghosts. The Tetum call the subterranean depths the *rai laran*, "the world inside." The secular world is known simply as *rai*, "the earth." The villagers have a word for "secular" *(sa'un)* and a term *(lulik)* which can be translated as "sacred," "prohibited," or "set apart." They seem to regard the sacred world as being a huge womb, a sort of great Earth Mother. In their system of cosmic classification, the Tetum associate men with the secular world and women with the sacred world. Since women belong to secular life as much as men, and are equally human, we might suppose the villagers to be contradictory in their classification. But some of their associations are not absolute. Relative, they switch with context. In ordinary life, which is regarded as secular, women like men are secular; but unlike men (who maintain their secular status regardless of context), in sacred rituals women become linked in villagers' minds with the sacred elements of the cosmos. Yet even within a ritual a woman's cosmic status can fluctuate. In the marriage rites the officiating woman may at one moment represent the sacred world and at the next the secular. As with sex, so with rank. In a secular situation, that is, in ordinary life, humans are superior to ghosts.

In a sacred situation, that is, in sacred ritual and myth, ghosts are superior. Consistent with these associations, in sacred rituals women are superior to men.

THE MYTH OF ORIGIN

Most villagers believe princedom society originated when three human beings clambered out of an object resembling a womb. Several myths recount in different ways what is supposed to have happened in those primeval times when the order which now governs society and the supernatural world was created. A "pregnant stone," the rear room (or "womb" or "tomb") of the house, the womb of a buffalo cow, or the sacred world itself, alternate as the birthplace of humanity in different origin myths. No "correct" variant exists. Such details of humanity's birth are unimportant. What matters is that sometime in the mythic past the first humans emerged from a womb-like receptacle. For Mamulak folk this receptacle was the earth itself, Mother Earth, the sacred world, the sacred womb. I first heard the story of this event from one of my most garrulous providers of data, Leal Soares' thirty-five-year-old daughter, Agostinha Soares, of Mane Hat.

Several local men wanted to marry Agostinha, but the prospect of working around the house or laboring in gardens for a husband mortified her, and unlike most women of her age she preferred to remain single. A hive of gossip, Agostinha was ever active in communal life. Of all villagers she was the least embarrassed by our first excursions to village homes, and we quickly became firm friends. Agostinha's popularity drew us into an ever-expanding network of people, and before long we were part of the local scene. Agostinha loved the spotlight. Flipping through our portfolio of Caraubalo photographs we were later much surprised to find how often she appears.

Photographs, incidentally, made a useful tool in our research. A camera made us welcome in almost everyone's house. Lining up an entire hamlet, Maxine would photograph its residents, and a few weeks later (after the prints had returned from the camera store in Dili) we would distribute copies to the hamlet residents, asking the names and kinship ties of each person in the picture. This technique simplified our task of identification, and made the villagers more willing to answer questions. Agostinha often took upon herself the job of preparing villagers for a picture-taking session. Whether she had close relatives in the hamlet or not no one ever seemed resentful. Experience taught us to seek her opinion whenever a scandal enriched the life of either Mamulak or Mane Hat, or some dispute shattered their peace. She never failed to uncover a likely cause, nor did she hesitate to forecast its outcome, though her talent as a clairvoyant rarely matched her skill as a political analyst. Well informed on ritual and myth, Agostinha narrated the Caraubalo tale of origin to us on March 14, 1967 in these words:

"When the world was created no humans existed; just the sea. Then two pieces of land appeared. One was in an area later to be known as Badiri; the other was in what was later to be Uma Kik [one of Caraubalo's neighbors]. Bit by bit other pieces emerged from the waters until the entire island of Timor lay stretched out. Two vaginas appeared in the ground. Each flanked the boundary separating Caraubalo from its northern neighbor, Loi Huno. Caraubalo's vagina was called Mahuma. Loi Huno's was Lequi Bui. From Mahuma clambered the ancestors of the present-day Caraubalo folk (except for the descendants of later immigrants). These primeval ancestors founded six Caraubalo villages: Mane Hat, Mamulak, Vessá, Cabira Oan, Hás Abut, and Lamaclaran. The seventh, Sira Lari, was established in the early years of this century. To clamber up out of the vagina, men and women pulled themselves over its lip with creepers from a certain species of tree. Their descendants venerate this tree and will neither cut nor eat its fruits. You can still see the Mahuma vagina. It's partly concealed by a huge "pregnant stone" round in shape. No one can open up the shaft that delves deeply into the earth. Those who first emerged from the sacred world became the founders of our aristocratic class. We call them the princedom landlords. There were three leaders. Rubi Rika and Lera Tiluk were brothers. Cassa Sonek was their sister. They and their descendants lived only in Mamulak and Mane Hat. Those who followed them out of the sacred womb were relegated to the commoner class and became their "tenants." Their descendants, the population of Vessá, Cabira Oan, Hás Abut, and Lamaclaran, remain in this condition today."

The British anthropologist Bronislaw Malinowski (1884–1942) would describe this story as a "charter" justifying contemporary institutions since it accounts for the status difference between aristocrats and commoners and confirms the religious belief that the Tetum Adam and Eve rose from the earth. This emergence villagers call by the same name they give their birth ritual: *sai rai*, "to leave the earth."

Such religious categories as ancestral ghost, spirit, and the sacred are "symbols." For the Tetum, as for other peoples, they appear not only in ritual, language, literature, and art, but also in material objects or artifacts (houses, clothing) and in nature (earth, water). We can define a symbol with Professor Victor Turner as "something visible, or tangible, or immediately available for human use standing for something less visible, or

22

less tangible, or less available." Anything can be symbolic: words, colors, actions, material artifacts, animals, humans, past events, and present events. Depending upon what they stand for or the use to which they are put, symbols may be either secular or sacred. Although many symbols are confined to a single culture, others appear on every inhabited continent, and in earlier cultures as well as in contemporary ones. Dr. Carl Jung (1875–1961), the Swiss psychoanalyst, suggested that every human being inherits certain mental impressions from his ancestors, much as he inherits his genetic traits. These impressions are universal symbols which he termed "archetypes." Blood, stones, the association between rooms, wombs, and tombs, and the association of the right hand with men and the left hand with women may be archetypes. So might that symbol known as the Earth Mother.

The symbolic classification of many societies equates rooms, wombs, and tombs. Only phonetically do they resemble one another in the English language, but some languages (such as Tetum) make their association so complete the same word denotes all three types of chamber. In Tetum the word is *lolon.* Their association helps us interpret one of the most important of all Tetum symbols, the sacred world. Connecting the secular world and the sacred world are vents. These limestone craters, which villagers call "vaginas" *(fona),* spatter the Caraubalo landscape. Varying from a couple of feet to several yards wide, they wind tortuously down into the sacred world. The largest is Mahuma. Any traveler in the princedom can stand on the lip of this gaping vent and gaze into its subterranean obscurity. Were he foolhardy enough to venture down into the dark void the climber would fall prey to the ancestral ghosts or other spiritual denizens of this region. No local would dare. The wombs of women and buffalo cows, the rear room of the house, and pregnant stones symbolize the sacred world. When a child is born, a buffalo cow is expected to give birth to a calf and a pregnant stone to give birth to a baby stone, while in the birth ritual the father must carry his newly born infant through the house vagina (the back door) into the world of kin (blood relatives) and *affines* (relatives by marriage) outside. Each birth commemorates the mythological emergence of the first humans from the Mahuma vagina. The most valued is that of the human baby. Its advent on the scene re-enacts the births of Rubi Rika, Lera Tiluk, and Cassa Sonek, which is why the Tetum call the birth ritual by a term which translates as "to leave the earth" *(sai rai).* This sacred world is a Timorese version of the Earth Mother archetype, which may have been prominent in the religions of Paleolithic societies, and which remains widespread today.

Having been born from the Earth Mother and a condition of sacredness, the three founders of Caraubalo started their secular lives on the earth's surface. When they died they re-entered the earth as dead souls which later evolved into ancestral ghosts. Sacred to secular and back to sacred: this is the cycle their descendants have repeated every generation (Figure 3). Human existence is cyclical. A person is born, not literally from the earth of course, but from his mother's womb. But the womb of the Earth Mother and that of the human mother are symbolically the same thing.

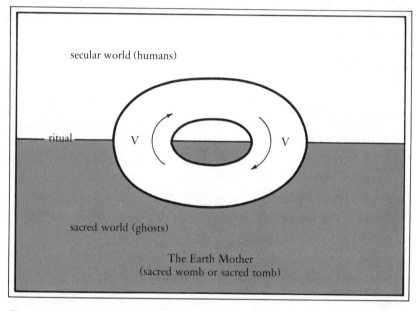

secular world (humans)

ritual

V   V

sacred world (ghosts)

The Earth Mother
(sacred womb or sacred tomb)

Figure 3 The Tetum Cycle of Human Existence. The letter V stands for the vagina of the Earth Mother and the opening to the tomb.

THE SACRED WORLD

Life begins for the individual when the soul assumes residence in his body, while that body is housed in its mother's womb. No one can say where the soul originates, but it keeps its link with the body for life. Sickness means some spiritual or pseudo-spiritual being has displaced it from the body for a temporary period. If the soul is prevented from returning, death results. The Tetum attribute death *(maté)* to the loss of the soul. The soul resides in the head. When it departs or an alien spirit shoves it out, its exits are the nostrils, mouth, or ears. Through these doors any invader also enters. "Soul" is *klamar.* Inside a living body it is *klamar moris (moris* means "alive" or "living"); outside a dead body, *klamar maté.* The Victorian scholar Edward Tylor's (1832–1917) famous description of the ghost-soul of non-literate peoples fits neatly the picture which the term "soul" conjures up in the imaginations of villagers. "It is," Tylor said, "a thin unsubstantial human image, in its nature a sort of vapour, film, or shadow" (1873:429). The soul is immortal. Wrenched from its body at death, for twelve months after the corpse has been interred the dead soul flits back and forth between the two worlds. It plagues the hamlet of its kin, causing illness and perhaps death, because it envies them. A final rite *(keta maté)* dispatches it to the sacred womb to join the ancestral ghosts and become one of them in time. Until this rite, the dead soul is only an occasional visitor to the sacred world, but the nether world's other occupants—demons, nature spirits, and ancestral ghosts—rarely leave. When they do, it is usually in response to deliberate urgings or accidental promptings from the world above.

Literally translated, the word *rai na'in* means "lord of the earth." It denotes two things: the aristocratic population of Caraubalo; and a class of spirits (demons) dwelling in the sacred world. These demons own such places in the secular world as a grove of bamboo, an old tree, or a lake. They enter the upper world at these spots and manifest themselves to passers-by. Unlike dead souls or ancestral ghosts, at no stage in its existence is a demon housed in its own material envelope; but it has the power to materialize for a time as a snake or a beautiful woman. Meeting a demon is usually disastrous, as the following story shows.

Several years before my arrival, a Mamulak elder, Loi Nahak, was walking to his garden three miles from his hamlet when he found his path barred by a lovely, dark-skinned girl. She was not from Caraubalo, so he feared the girl was a demon. To stop Loi from running she took hold of his hand and invited him to make love. Too stiff with fright to refuse, he lay down in her arms. When he arrived home that evening Dau Nahak, his wife, sensed all was not well but said nothing. During the night a gigantic female python slid into their bedroom, bewitched Dau into not waking up, and obliged Loi Nahak to copulate. With the coming of dawn the python returned to the sacred world. The next day Dau's suspicions made her think of divorce. She and her husband began sleeping in different rooms, and shortly afterwards the marriage broke up.

Unlike other spirits and a class of creatures partly human yet partly spirit called "witches," nature spirits are never directly harmful. Although they fertilize plants, these spirits are the servants of the ghosts, who command them. Only by not making a union fertile can a nature spirit injure human beings. To prevent a spirit withholding assistance wives offer sacrifices during rituals to nature spirits and to ghosts. Three main categories of nature spirit exist: the buffalo spirit, corn spirit and rice spirit. Each category includes many individual spirits. Exactly how many, no one knows.

Of all the inhabitants of the sacred world, the most plentiful are the souls of persons who died over two generations back. These are ancestral ghosts. Souls of persons who would be grandparents, parents, or members of a villager's own generation are still classed as dead souls. The process whereby a dead soul becomes an ancestral ghost is a mystery.

Caraubalo has nine clans. Clans in non-literate societies belong to a widespread form of social corporation known as descent groups. *A descent group is a group of persons of both sexes who trace their ancestry (descent) from a common founder.* The largest type of descent group, the clan usually recognizes as its founder a fabulous person, a mythological animal, or some object which in biological reality could never have performed this task. Clans are frequently justified in creation myths and have "totems." *A totem is something which is exclusively regarded as the property of a particular clan and which plays a crucial part in its identity.* Quite often a clan's totem is the founder. This is especially likely if that founder was a mythological animal or object. The founder of one of the two clans which make up Mamulak was an eel *(tuna).* The eel is both founder and totem. It is taboo (forbidden) for any member of Tuna clan to kill or eat an eel. Its origin is described in a creation myth which I tell in chapter 5. During clan rituals Tuna kinsfolk wear designs painted to resemble an eel on their bodies. Mamulak's second clan is Ina-Aman. It also has its creation myth, totem, and taboo.

Many societies with clans divide each into a number of lineages. In the Tetum language, lineages are called *feto fuan, mane fuan.* This expression translates as "the fruit of the woman and the fruit of the man." This poetic image is consistent with the themes of the native symbolism. Husband and wife copulate, and from their union a new creature, or creation, emerges. The union of opposites which are complementary makes creation possible. Lineages are always smaller in population than clans, and though all the lineages of a clan share the same fabulous founder, totem, and taboo, the founder of each lineage is invariably a credible person. While dietary restriction, kinship rights and duties, and behavior may distinguish the lineages of a clan, they all share the same (clan) totem. Tuna clan consists of three lineages: Bua Laran, Baria Laran, and Cailulik. An eel created the clan, but each lineage was founded by a human being. The founders were brothers, the sons of a man called Léla-sou, who became involved with the eel. Each Mamulak and Mane Hat lineage ideally corresponds to a hamlet, but factional conflicts and over-population have forced most lineages to spread themselves over several hamlets. The smallest social grouping is the household, which consists of the simple family, or nuclear family, and various dependents. The simple family itself contains the parents and unmarried children.

All persons belonging to the same clan are known in anthropological usage as *kin*, or *agnates*. Relatives by marriage are called *affines*. The Caraubalo Tetum lack a term for "affine."

In Western cultures, Catholics believe that their Church has two classes of members: the living members ("the Church visible") and those who have died ("the Church invisible"). The dead members are the souls in Heaven or Purgatory. The Tetum hold much the same kind of belief, except that they have no notion of Purgatory or Heaven, and apply this dual way of classifying their members to their clans. Each clan has two types of kinsfolk: ancestral ghosts and their living descendants. Just as a clansperson has the right to demand help from a living kinsperson, so he can invoke a dead kinsperson, that is, an ancestral ghost, to assist him. Such help usually requires ghosts to send nature spirits into the gardens to make the union of seed and soil productive, or to ensure that a husband fertilizes his wife when they copulate. Such requests are made in prayers uttered during birth and marriage rituals at the household altar, or ritual shelf, and at altars found in the garden or near forest paths. Ghosts are also entitled to food, wine, and other offerings. To ignore their needs invites sterile unions, sickness and death.

In 1960, believing it to be haunted by their ancestral ghosts, the agnates of Bua Laran lineage abandoned the hamlet their ancestors had founded many generations ago. They had neglected to offer ritual sacrifices to the ghosts, despite their ritual obligation, and so their ancestors had decided to punish them. One reason the Tetum are not particularly worried about the menace facing them from the soul of a recently deceased person is they know their ghosts will help protect them from its spite. I was not a member of any clan and had no ancestors to defend me when I approached Cai Tuli's coffin, which was why Leal Soares was anxious. When the ghosts withdraw their protection, their living kin can throw up ritual defenses against the marauding dead soul, but the close kin of the deceased are more vulnerable than before. The Bua Laran ghosts withdrew support; unhampered by ghostly resistance, they looked on as the dead souls of the hamlet's deceased residents harassed the lineage.

Soon nightmares, allegations of nocturnal suffocation, and nightly hysteria threw the hamlet into confusion. After a while even the ancestral ghosts began persecuting residents. Night after night souls sobbed and ghosts whispered balefully from the dark jungle, and though dozens of rituals were performed to appease the ancestors all was to no avail. Months dragged unhappily on until one evening as they were returning from their gardens, some demoralized Bua Laran agnates spied what they took to be an ancestral ghost. They described it later to their fellows back at the hamlet as a female. Swaying from side to side, she was plodding toward them on stubby legs. Black hair hid her face, and a loincloth hung from her waist; her arms looked incredibly long and powerful. Details of the strange encounter were embellished with the telling and retelling, and before many nights had passed sleepers began waking up at night screaming they were being throttled to death by ghostly hands. These hallucinations proved the final straw for nerves already stretched to breaking point, and in a despairing attempt to atone for their sins the Bua Laran kin re-sited their hamlet a short distance away. They were troubled no longer.

It may seem incredible that a community of rational persons could permit itself to be so wracked by hysteria as to quit a venerated plot of land bequeathed it by sacred ancestors centuries before; but as the nineteen executions for witchcraft in Salem, Massachusetts, during 1692 demonstrate, mass delusion is not confined to non-literate peoples. Any community under pressure can erupt into a swirling cauldron of wild accusations involving moral offenses, and sightings of impossible creatures or far-fetched objects (consider flying saucers) are typical. Since the early 1950's Caraubalo princedom had been steadily acculturated by Portuguese missionaries and civil servants, who represented a European power that had been on Timor for over four hundred years. Acculturation had been spearheaded by the Catholic missionaries, who intensified the proseltyzing begun (though carried through fitfully) in the late sixteenth century. They started by attacking the native religion, with the result that many younger villagers jettisoned the faith of their fathers and neglected to perform rituals. With a core of native Christians at the outset, Bua Laran lineage was in the forefront of these changes; and when its first few members began complaining about nocturnal sicknesses their more conservative neighbors as well as those who had begun to "move with the times" were able to wallow in guilt for having allowed the new religious ideas to destroy traditional dogma. Once the idea that their ghosts were perfectly justified in punishing them had won a hold over their emotions, everything the least bit unusual in the hamlet and its surroundings was interpreted as ghostly retribution. The few who remained more rational were caught up in this collective delirium, and only the trauma of a forced migration could end the panic.

Ancestors come in two sexes. The sacred world has males as well as females. But so dominant are ancestral women over their men that when glimpsed by human beings, ghosts are invariably female in appearance. And in the secular world women usually preside over sacred rituals. One exception is the ritual of birth.

THE RITUAL OF BIRTH

Anthropologists have argued for years over how to define the term "ritual." Basically, two choices are available. The first includes some reference to the sacred. Thus for Victor Turner, ritual is *"prescribed formal behavior for occasions not given over to technological routine, having reference to beliefs in mystical beings or powers"* (1967:19). The second makes no distinction between sacred and secular. Adapting Turner's definition gives us, *"prescribed formal behavior for occasions not given over to technological routine."* Professor Edmund Leach (1966) would follow this definition. Shaking hands would not be a ritual act for Turner unless in some way it involved "mystical beliefs or powers"; for Leach, it would. Provided the user makes clear which definition he follows, either is valid.

I shall use the term "ritual" in Leach's sense, to cover what we can then classify as either secular or sacred rituals. Since most of the rituals described in this book are sacred rituals, the term "ritual" from now on refers to sacred rituals only. Unlike sacred rituals, secular ones make no reference to "mystical beings or powers," but both categories of ritual are only ideal types. Very rarely can the anthropologist stick an exclusive label on a particular ritual and class it without qualification as, say, a secular ritual. Like the Caraubalo rituals of birth, marriage, and death, rituals in all societies normally contain elements of both. The problem is to decide whether the primary intention of the ritual or the main elements which compose it are predominately secular or sacred. Because ancestral ghosts and dead souls attend the Tetum rituals, birth, marriage, and death, I class each as sacred.

Rituals can also be classed according to whether they make things happen or merely commemorate what has occurred in the past. The marriage, corn, and death rituals belong in the first category: either they bring together humans and ghosts (or nature spirits), or they separate things which are secular from those that are sacred. Because they are instruments for change, we can call them *instrumental rituals.* Rituals which commemorate a mythical event and express ideas and symbolic themes, such as the birth ritual, belong in the second category—that of *expressive rituals.* Again we must not be too strict about slotting a given ritual into an "expressive" or "instrumental" pigeonhole. Most have elements of both.

Of all the Tetum rituals, the most important are those we can describe as both instrumental and sacred. These can be grouped as rituals of union, or rituals of separation. By uniting ancestral ghosts (or nature spirits) with human beings, rituals of union create human babies, plants, political harmony, social peace, health, and other productive benefits. Most Tetum rituals fall into this class. They also conform to a theme which runs through collective thought and ritual behavior as well as appearing in the kinship systems and architecture of the house — "union-leading-to-creation." By separating secular from sacred, rituals of separation conform to a second major theme of this culture — "separation-leading-to-restoration." When creatures from the two opposite worlds unite outside ritual—that is to say, when the act of union is not under human control, disorder or chaos results. As in the Bua Laran drama, in the human world this disorder is symbolized by sickness and death. The proper abode of ghosts and dead souls is the sacred womb, so that outside ritual their presence in the secular world destroys the neat dual order of native thinking. Ghosts and humans assume each others' properties. Ghosts, which in an ordered universe are invisible and intangible, become visible and tangible; yet they remain ghosts. Humans, by behaving in bizarre or abnormal ways, assume a strangeness associated in Tetum minds with the sacred world. To restore the order of traditional thinking these properties must be, as it were, returned to their proper owners; this return is precisely what the two major rituals of separation—exorcism and death—accomplish. They *restore* the cosmic order first established in mythic times.

Although containing elements of union and separation, the birth ritual is mainly an expressive, sacred ritual. Like marriage and death, it begins in the house. Inside the house womb, extending from ground to roof in the middle of the rear half of the room, is a thick central pillar. I call it the "ritual pillar." Here ghosts and their human kin unite. Encircling the pillar about four feet from the floor is the household altar, or ritual shelf, a wooden affair a few inches in diameter. One corner of the room has a rectangular fireplace containing a hearth, which consists of three rounded stones placed tripod fashion at the center of a tray smothered with ash. Food is cooked in a fire burning between the stones or in pots perched on them. Mats plaited from dried, shredded palm-tree leaves clothe the bare, split bamboo floors. On one such mat, somewhere between pillar and hearth, a pregnant woman gives birth.

An experienced older woman acts as midwife. Her dexterity critically regarded by as many hamlet women as the room will hold, the midwife nips the umbilical cord to leave roughly three inches dangling from the belly. This cord is known by the same name as that denoting a descent group *(cain)*, which also means "stalk" or "stem." The three inches drop off in their own good time. In its mother's womb the infant has been living in the sacred world represented in symbolic form, and spectators to this drama interpret the act of cutting the cord as equivalent to severing the tie binding the infant to this spiritual existence. Henceforth, until death, this human being will be a creature of the secular world. The need to keep up (ritual) contact with the sacred world's inhabitants is symbolized by what follows. The midwife stuffs that part of the cord she has cut off into a small pouch which the father has previously plaited from palm-leaves. She adds the afterbirth to it, and fastens the pouch to the ritual pillar, at a spot slightly above the altar. The stained birth cloths and other soiled material she drops on the ritual shelf itself. As a "bridge" between the two worlds, the ritual pillar is an apt place for these symbols of the productive benefits which derive from humans and ancestral ghosts uniting.

Most Mamulak and Mane Hat folk descend from Rubi Rika, Lera Tiluk, and Cassa Sonek. As we saw in the myth of birth or origin, they believe a creeper of a certain species of tree enabled them to scramble into the secular world, and so this tree is their totem. Other Caraubalo clans trace their origins either to persons who followed these three out of the earthy vagina by using other plants as ropes, or to immigrants from other, neighboring princedoms. We can now see the connection between descent groups, umbilical cords, stalks, and stems—and why all four things are covered by the single word *cain*. A descent group binds the individual to his primeval origins, to the sacred world and to his ghostly clan ancestors.

Five days after the withered remnants of the cord drop off his body, a boy is carried from the house womb in his father's arms. A girl is taken out four days after her cord falls. The midwife places the cord in a second pouch, which she also attaches to the ritual pillar. When the morning chosen for the birth ritual dawns, the father takes his child from the mother, carries it through the house vagina into the hamlet plaza where a mat lies on the ground. As his own clansfolk and those of his wife surge forward to glimpse the infant, the man gently deposits it on the mat. The father's clan provided the marriage gifts or *bridewealth* which was needed to obtain the wife. Its members are the wife-takers. The wife's clan is the wife-giving descent group. The baby is the concrete symbol of the creative benefits that derive from the two groups forming an affinal bond, and from the husband and wife establishing a sexual bond. Birth is an occasion for both groups to come together. Represented by the father, the wife-takers symbolize the sacred world of ancestral ghosts. Represented by two young bachelors, the wife-givers symbolize the secular world of human beings.

While those women who reside in the hamlet chop wood, start fires, pound corn, and in other ways begin preparations for making food, the two bachelors give a pig and a piece of red cloth to the father. This cloth is sacred. It has two alternative names: the *hena lolon*, and the *hena mêan tahan ida*. (The name *hena mêan tahan ida* I discuss in detail in chapter 4; *hena lolon* translates as "the womb of cloth.") By wrapping the child in it, the father makes another (womb-like) symbol of the sacred world before re-entering his house. Inside, he unwraps the cloth from about the child's body, drops the cloth on the floor just below the ritual shelf, and slips the infant into its mother's arms. Before rejoining the crowd in the plaza the father takes a little rice from one of the women in the house and puts it on the ritual shelf. In a couple of prayers muttered to the ghosts of Rubi Rika, Lera Tiluk, and Cassa Sonek, the man tries to persuade them to add further children to his clan. By this prayer the man acts out the link his religion makes between wife-takers and ancestral ghosts.

As soon as the husband steps into the plaza, one of his sisters (if he has none, any woman from his clan will do) enters the house womb. She takes up the pouch with the cord and afterbirth, the birth cloths, and the pouch containing the other part of the umbilical cord. These she stuffs into a dry water pitcher made of clay, which she carries through the house vagina. She puts the pitcher on a plaited palm-leaf ring resting on her head, and sets forth into the jungle to her clan's shrine, which is usually about a half a mile from the hamlet. Acting as escorts, the two bachelors walk ahead of her. In secular life, when men and women travel together, the women precede the men. Like the husband performing the birth offering to his ancestral ghosts, however, this is a case of *ritual reversal*, that is, a situation in which roles and symbolic associations are opposite to what they are normally. The names by which the three address one another as they chatter on the return journey suggest why. The woman calls the men "Rubi" and "Lera"; they call her "Cassa." Just as the two brothers Rubi Rika and Lera Tiluk escorted their sister from out of the Mahuma vagina, so the two male actors in this dramatic re-enactment of the Caraubalo myth of origin lead the woman from her hamlet. In the story, they bring her forth into the world to help create princedom society. In the ritual, they escort her to the symbol of her descent group society—the clan shrine.

Figure 4 shows the clan shrine to consist of four parts: the pregnant stones, table stones, the fruit tree and St. Domingo's tree, and the bamboo pole *(ai suak)* and coconut shell.

The pregnant stones. These three rounded stones (numbers 2, 3, and 4 in the Figure) are light pink in color. Each symbolizes the sacred world. Villagers figuratively describe them as the "source" *(u'e)* of the clan and buffalo herd. The shrine is sometimes called the "buffalo shrine" because

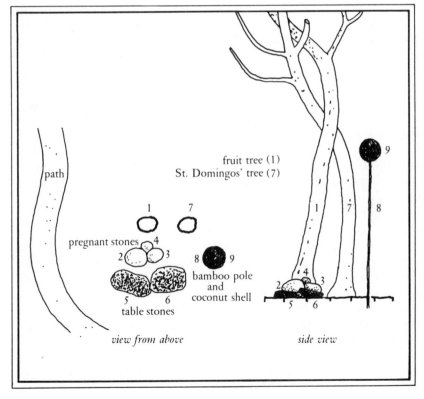

Figure 4   The clan shrine

33

of this, and the stones regarded as the source of "baby" stones. As we saw in the myth of origin, a pregnant stone of far greater dimensions than any of these three hangs over the Mahuma vagina. The shrine's centerpiece, these stones house visiting ghosts. Most venerated is number 2, which is slightly larger than its companions and is the most popular lodging for spiritual visitors. When Maxine and I examined the Tuna clan shrine this stone was partly buried in the soil, so we found it difficult to estimate its size. I would guess it was about the size of a soccer ball. Only the clan priestess is permitted by the ghosts to touch a pregnant stone, and even she cannot take one in her hand. All the stones are female.

The table stones. The flat table stones, numbers 5 and 6, lie behind the pregnant stones. Stone 5 symbolizes the secular world. Its opposite, stone 6, stands for the sacred world. Each measures two square feet in area and is about two inches thick. Both are black. Unlike pregnant stones, these can be handled with impunity. One afternoon Hílda Pereira lifted them for my benefit, and disclosed a foundation of tiny stones.

The trees. Tree number 1, a fruit tree, has a black bark. Its companion, number 7, is the tree of St. Domingo; when sliced away, its green bark reveals wood of the same shade of pink as the pregnant stones. This bark supplies ingredients for medicines used by the local shaman to make wounds heal more rapidly.

The bamboo pole and coconut shell. Strictly speaking, the Tetum word *ai suak* refers only to the dibble, or digging stick, used for planting seeds. Here it applies to its ritual equivalent, a bamboo pole (number 8) six feet long and an inch in diameter stuck into the soil at one end and impaling a coconut shell (number 9) at the other. When pole and shell decay they are replaced by the priestess. The point at which the pole enters the earth is called the vagina, a term also applied to each of the three nodes by which a coconut is attached to its branch. Through one of these nodes the sharpened pole is rammed. The pole symbolizes a man's penis, which thus enters two "vaginas." One is in the soil and the other is in the coconut. Here we have an impacted symbol of union. Standing at the shrine of the clan, the group of humans which gives cultural life to an individual, it impresses upon the minds of all who see it the native belief that life depends upon the union of man and woman, and of human beings and ancestral ghosts. Without these unions, creation would not be possible. The clan would die out, and in fact could never have come into being in the first place. What could be more appropriate than that three persons representing the two sexes, a wife-giving group and a wife-taking group, and the founders of Caraubalo should perform part of the birth ritual at this hallowed shrine?

Arriving at the shrine, one of the men takes the pitcher from the woman's head and shins up the fruit tree with the pitcher of birth relics in one hand. He ties it to a convenient branch and slides down. The pitcher is left to disintegrate and its contents to decay. As noted earlier, the umbilical cord symbolizes the bond linking the baby with its ancestral ghosts and clan. The pitcher represents the mother's womb. Stuffing the cord inside the pitcher and tying both to the clan shrine are acts reminding villagers that this latest clan member, though now a secular being, remains bound to the sacred world. Their ritual performance of the creation myth completed, the woman leads the way home.

At the hamlet the bachelors enter the front door of the father's house, and wrap the infant in its cloth "womb." One man carries it through the vagina of the house and places it on the mat. No sooner does he straighten up than the father's kin and those of the mother noisily scramble to line up on opposite sides of the mat. Aroused by the commotion starting up in the plaza, the mother steps from the house to join her clan. Both groups begin hurling insults at each other, and throw fruit, corn cobs, and debris from the fire which is by now blazing away. They take great care no missile flies near the baby. For a while the hamlet is in such uproar violence seems about to break out. Near its climax women from both sides run to nearby pitchers full of water, dip their hands into them, and return to splash everyone in sight. When no dry bodies are left they stop running back and forth to the pitchers for water, and the hubbub dies away.

Why this confrontation? To begin with, water is another symbol of sexual and cosmic union; the indigenous word for "water" is the same as the word for "source" (u'e). Like other ritual offerings, sprinkling water stands for the bringing together of humans and ghosts for procreative ends. This is why women douse water over wife-givers and wife-takers. But you can only bring together things which are separate to start with, which explains the taunts and insults the two groups exchange. This hostile behavior is a small rite of separation, performed to stress the fact that both groups, though mutually interdependent, are nonetheless distinct and separate—just like men and women, just like humans and ghosts.

Now comes the feast. While they eat, the celebrants keep a close watch on the infant. The clamour will almost certainly have kept it awake, but long before everyone has eaten his fill its little eyelids will droop. Taking her cue, the mother leaves the feast, lifts the tiny bundle into her arms, and lays it to rest in the house. Given any luck, for the night's events have scarcely begun, the child will slumber till morning.

After stomachs have expanded more than usual and more drinks than are compatible with strict sobriety drunk, younger spinsters clear the table and begin washing up the dirty crockery. Kin and affines get together in small groups and gossip fills the night air.

One indulgence the people of Timor share with many other Asian folk is betel-chewing, about which they are as compulsive as tobacco-smoking Westerners. A leaf from a betel tree is sprinkled with powdered lime. The leaf is twisted tightly to prevent the powder filtering out, and together with one or two slices of areca nut, is stuffed into the mouth. A minute's chewing produces a spittle ("areca blood") ranging in color from bright scarlet to brown. Mildy narcotic, this mixture is pleasant enough once the neophyte has learned how to clear his throat without spitting the red, frothy mass down his shirt, where the stains set stubbornly. Betel-chewing is an essential component of most Tetum rituals, but its sole purpose on birth-ritual nights is to encourage relaxation. When gossip slackens, story-tellers take up their narratives, and as contented hours slip away narrators impress their audience with the deeds of fabulous heroes, or amuse them by recounting some of the adventures of Monkey, Dog, Crocodile, and other popular creatures of the Caraubalo literary bestiary, or thrill them with horror stories. As one narrator flags, another takes his place. Birth rituals attract smaller crowds than death rituals, and fewer storytellers, and so they usually break up well before dawn.

Two or three days later the parents name their child. Unlike many societies, the Tetum lack a ritual of name-giving. The parents simply pick the name of a kinsperson or affine they admire, and link it to the father's first name and that of his clan. Suppose a couple selects "Fahi" as their son's first name, and the father (who belongs to the Tuna clan) is Lequi Nahak Tuna. The son will be called Fahi Lequik Tuna. A "K" always ends the paternal name when it becomes the second name of a child. Girls' names differ from those given to boys, but are assigned identically. The mother cannot usually pass on her first name nor that of her clan to a daughter. If an infant cries too much or rejects its mother's milk the parents conclude it disapproves of their choice of first name. So they change it.

Ritual never duplicates myth exactly, and each medium of communication takes advantage of symbols the other neglects. But both in their distinctive ways proclaim to members of Caraubalo that humanity is born from a sacred womb into a secular world through a vagina of some kind. The ancestral ghost's territory is a region villagers know little about.

The depths of the sacred womb are unfathomable for secular creatures, including anthropologists. But the world Rubi Rika, Lera Tiluk, Cassa Sonek, Léla-sou, and their descendants have prepared for the latest recruit to Tetum society is open for inspection.

Ecology

3

When his tongue had been sufficiently lubricated by wine Rubi Loik could gush information like Agostinha, but his interpretation of daily events, at least insofar as he was involved, was too far out of joint with general opinion to be considered reliable. Still, he knew much about the institutions of Mamulak, and we got to know him quite well. Fifty-year old Rubi Loik was the head of the only household in the smallest of the three hamlets of Cailulik lineage, one of three lineages into which the Tuna clan is divided. He always explained that he lived apart from his fellows to reduce the danger of inter-household squabbling over stolen chickens. His neighbors held the view that no one outside his own household would tolerate his presence. Them I believe.

Even among a people lacking a Protestant work ethic, Rubi was notorious for laziness. Regardless of others, he would often fall silent when a dark mood struck him, speaking again only when ready. Misunderstandings continually jarred his interpersonal relationships, and Rubi was said to be the most quarrelsome of all the Mamulak villagers. Rubi Loik's residential status was ambiguous. Born and raised in Mamulak, he had once emigrated to his married son's village in Uma Kik princedom, but had returned to settle down in Mamulak. Maxine and I were fond of Rubi, and he evidently liked us too, for he invited us to be the godparents of his infant daughter, Siba. We promptly agreed, but some weeks later, after learning Maxine was not a Catholic ("is not a

Christian"), Rubi retracted his offer. We never could discover the identities of the eventual godparents. Siba probably remains unbaptized, for her father was a singularly stubborn and unself-conscious follower of the old religion. His offer may have been a political tactic, though I don't know what he thought to gain. Rubi had early doubts about us. Three months after we first met him he wanted to know if it was really true we had come to the island to study Tetum and the ways of its speakers; had I not, perhaps, been abandoned by my own kin and left to wander all over the secular world? I was glad to put him right.

Like every Caraubalo resident Rubi Loik had his own idiosyncrasies, but he was the product of the same conditions which had molded the lives of his fellows. First, there was the Tetum culture which every resident (the origin myth to the contrary) had inherited from peoples who migrated from the mainland of Southeast Asia sometime before 1,000 A.D. No scholar knows much about them, except that present-day villagers inherited their language from them. Second, he was subject to the influence exercised by neighboring peoples of other cultures, chiefly the Portuguese. Third, he was bound to the land, which influences the daily and annual life styles of the Timorese. Shiftless though he might be, Rubi Loik was as much under its control as the most industrious of his neighbors. One of his gardens was near my house, and I was well placed to study many of his yearly activities; I use him here as an example of how his people have adapted themselves to the physical environment of Timor. I have another reason for selecting Rubi. His attachment to his religion made him carry out the rituals which are part of Tetum ecology with a thoroughness many families lack, so I was able to learn from an enthusiastic believer.

PHYSICAL ENVIRONMENT

The climate and landscape of Timor are such as to be found in the novels of Somerset Maugham or Joseph Conrad. Indeed, Conrad's *Victory* contains a reference (starkly unflattering) to Dili. The island, which is about three hundred miles long, has a mountainous backbone rising to eight thousand feet. This is flanked by a northern and a southern coast, which in eastern Timor display contrasting landscapes. The northern coast, which abuts the "feminine sea" (so-called because it is relatively calm), ends in most places in swamps or enters the sea in cliffs. The southern coast, which abuts the "masculine sea" (a violent stretch of water), consists of an undulating plain extending inland. Caraubalo (Figure 1) lies

Caraubalo Basin, as seen from Baria Laran and looking
northward toward a gap in the mountainous backbone of
eastern Timor. The coconut trees, savanna and bamboo-
fenced garden are typical of the Basin.

where this plain merges into the uplands, a transition exerting profound
influence on the local ecology. Another natural factor is the climatic cycle.
Little annual variation in temperature occurs, which means that the
climatic cycle *is* the rainfall cycle. Two wet seasons (November–January
and March–June) and two dry seasons (February and July–October) help
determine the Tetum seasonal cycle of economic, kinship, and ritual activities. Figure 5 summarizes the relationship between these variables. In
areas where soil conditions and relief are favorable, the heavy rainfall
coupled with the consistently high temperatures (80 to 90 degrees F.)
have produced dense stands of tropical forest with such species as teak,
casuarina, mahogany, palm trees, sago, and ironwood. At lower elevations
or where the soil is poorer, savanna replaces forest. In places it stretches
for miles. As befits a zone of topographic and ecological transition,
Caraubalo has a mixture of forest and savanna.

40

	November	December	January	February	March	April	May	June	July	August	September	October
Climate	WET		DRY		WET				DRY			
Horticulture	corn planted; most other crops planted; weeding	weeding	weeding	corn harvested	rice planted; weeding	corn planted; most other crops planted; weeding	weeding; bird scaring	weeding; bird scaring		rice harvested; areca harvested	corn harvested	garden dug and fired
		other crops harvested as necessary							most other crops harvested			
											garden fired	
Household location	garden	mainly hamlet	mainly hamlet	garden	garden	mainly garden	mainly hamlet	mainly garden	hamlet	hamlets and gardens	hamlets and gardens	mainly garden
Social activities	a few marriages	making cloth and implements; some visiting		no visiting	little visiting		much visiting		much visiting	marriages; housebuilding	visiting	

Figure 5 The seasonal cycle in Caraubalo

THE SEASONAL CYCLE

Tetum economy is based on the slash-and-burn, or swidden, cultivation of corn, sweet potatoes, yams, green vegetables of various kinds, and dry rice; and the rearing of pigs, as well as occasional buffaloes and horses. Corn and pigs dominate crops and livestock. Apart from coconuts (grown among the forest trees), all crops are cultivated in gardens. A garden is owned by members of a household, a group which may have from one to four gardens. At least one will be located near the household's hamlet. The others may be scattered about the countryside miles apart. Rubi Loik owned three gardens, which meant that he and his household, like everyone else, did more walking than they wanted. Rubi's household was composed of himself, his wife Sei Umau, two sons, and four daughters.

Before I describe the yearly cycle of activity I must first give a description of the corn shrine, for it is here that the most important agricultural ritual takes place. This ritual is the corn ritual—an essential feature of the annual cycle of work.

At the center of every garden is a complex of poles, stones, ferns, holes in the ground, and wooden debris. This is the corn shrine, the secular home of the corn spirit. For seeds to germinate and produce a rich harvest, this spirit must be induced to leave the sacred world and seek temporary shelter within the shrine. From the shrine the spirit can then enter the soil to fertilize the union of soil and seed. A ritual of union in which secular (masculine) fuses creatively with sacred (feminine) must be performed. A household failing to carry out the corn ritual risks crop failure. The name given this ritual (*halo batar moris*) tells us much about it. *Halo* is a verb meaning "to create"; *batar* is "corn." The verb *moris* is related to a term for the expression "to give birth to," and in its own right translates as "to live." This ritual "gives birth and life to the corn." To plant corn the gardeners dig holes (vaginas) two inches deep into which they drop three seeds. The number three symbolizes union. The term for seed is the same as that for human sperm, and when each hole is covered up with soil a concentrated picture of sexual (*male-female*) and cosmic (*human-spirit*) union is formed before the eyes of the laborers. It is no accident that the verb for "to plant" (*Kuda*) is the same as that "to copulate" or "to fuse sexually."

Like most shrines, Rubi Loik's was simple. (See Figure 6.) Thrown across and between three flat stones piled on top of one another were stems and leaves of a fern known as "water leaf." These were cut from the parent plant, taken to the shrine, and dropped into the positions shown. Throughout the year, as they aged and lost their red and green hues they were replaced by fresh cuttings. Around the stones lie pieces of bamboo

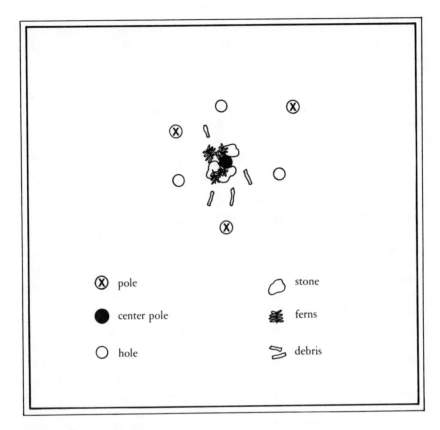

Figure 6   The corn shrine

cups destroyed in previous rituals. Encircling the stones, and around the imaginary circumference of a circle, were three holes each about one inch in diameter representing three "vaginas." Rubi made them with his dibble. Outside this inner triad was a second one, with three-foot-high dibbles stuck into the soil instead of holes. When they fall apart they are replaced by fresh ones. At the center of the shrine, surrounded by the three stones, was the fourth dibble, the center pole. Capping the shaved distal end of this dibble was a coconut shell, inserted on top just before the corn ritual began. As Rubi carefully pressed the dibble into one of the three natural holes at the base of the shell, Sei Umau (as the household priestess) sprinkled coconut water taken from the nut onto and around the shrine. This ablution is called *hissik* ("to give life to"). The dibble and coconut shell are virtually identical to the pole and shell of the clan shrine. Rubi could have used a bamboo pole, but he thought a dibble tougher than bamboo. So in the corn shrine we have another compact, intensive, image of union at the very place where humans (led by their ritual commander, the priestess) and a sacred being (the corn spirit) were to meet.

On the morning of the day Rubi Loik had selected for the performance of the rites his wife and children accompanied him to their nearest garden. He clambered up a nearby coconut tree, cut the three holes in the nut he had chosen, and poured the liquid into a bamboo cup Sei Umau held in her left hand. Why her left, and not her right hand is a matter worth explaining.

In a 1909 essay, Robert Hertz (1882–1915) pointed out that in many cultures the two hands symbolize ideas that are dually organized. The right hand is associated with superiority, goodness, men, and the secular; the left hand is mentally linked with their opposites. Since Hertz's time fieldwork has proved the universality of these associations. Among some peoples the right-left contrast even pre-empts the central status of the more widespread pairs, secular-sacred, humans-ghosts and men-women. When a woman acts as a priestess she represents the sacred world, and so relates to her husband and other mortals with her "sacred" hand. But when, as a human being, she represents her social group and the secular world to the spirits, she relates herself to them not with her left hand (which would offer a sterile union of left with left, female with female, sacred with sacred) but with her right (secular, masculine) hand. The use to which this contrast is put is relative, a relativity nowhere more apparent or more critical than in the functions Tetum symbolism assigns to women. As noted in chapter 2, a woman is both secular and sacred. Which of these properties is stressed depends upon the role she is required to play in a particular ritual or in different stages of the same ritual.

Back at Rubi's shrine, the empty coconut shell was set to one side as Sei Umau walked around the shrine sprinkling the liquid on it again. Since the coconut water (like betel spittle, ordinary water, and blood) also symbolizes the secular and sacred united, by this action she was initiating contact with the corn spirit, forming a bridge between its world and hers. Once this bridge has been established verbal communication is possible, and nourishment offered the visitor from the sacred world. While sprinkling the water the priestess chants a prayer assuring the spirit that enough food and drink for its needs will be provided during the time the corn is growing. She reminds it that coconut liquid represents the successful union of humans with spirits, secular with sacred, men with women, and seed with soil. The males remain silent. The prominence of men, always blatant in ordinary life, has vanished. For the moment, women are in charge; they and the spirits are superior to men and humanity.

Sei Umau ordered her husband to replace the old shell at the top of the dibble with the newly cut one. After he had obeyed, from her right hand she dropped a sack eight inches long and two inches wide on top of the stones. This sack is an analogue of the womb. Inside are three tiny cobs which symbolize the human baby, the product of the sexual union of man and woman—another symbol of the fertile union of opposites. After dropping the sack in place Sei Umau led her family to the hut every household has in each garden, while younger persons made a meal of rice, and the liver, heart, and entrails of a chicken. A large and wealthy household would kill a pig. Rubi's contented itself with this more modest offering. The Loiks ate most of the food, but left some. During the meal Sei Umau walked over to the shrine, in which the spirit was believed to have taken up residence, and tossed the leftovers onto the stones. She next sprinkled the chicken's blood from the bamboo cup over the stones, smashed it up and scattered the pieces around the shrine. Finally she returned to the house. For that garden the corn ritual was over.

Occasionally throughout the wet season Rubi, Sei, or one of their children would drop a little food on the shrine as they passed by the garden. Some villagers told us the spirit eats the food and drinks the blood. Rubi's theory was that the visitor only imbibes the "spirit" of the offerings. The details were of no concern to the villagers. What mattered most was that humans and a sacred being had entered into a creative relationship profitable for both. We have already witnessed the fear ghosts can inspire. But fear is not a feature of this particular association, even though the corn spirit is from another world, because the union is controlled by humans. The only emotion the spirit seems to inspire is anxiety that it may double-cross its human partners and refuse to make the fusion of seed and soil creative. As the corn grows the spirit keeps visiting its shrine to ensure a dead soul does not injure the crop. All being well, it returns to its natural home in the sacred womb. Should food offerings cease during this period, the spirit remains in the world below and the crop dies. Apart from the cooking, Rubi's household repeated this ritual at each of their garden shrines. They offered food from the original meal to the second and third corn spirits, but instead of blood (it congeals too rapidly to permit transportation) they gave betel spittle. Having, they hoped, persuaded the corn spirit to make the future crop fertile, the family had only to await the light rains which herald the onset of the wet season.

Figure 5 summarizes Rubi Loik's seasonal cycle, which was both the

ideal and roughly the norm. The season beginning in 1965 had been untypical. The rains came in early November, halted for two weeks, then
recommenced. As a result, the seeds implanted in the soil during the first
downpours failed to germinate. The 1966–1967 season was satisfactory.
Let me describe it here as an average year.

In early November, two weeks after Rubi's family had returned
home from their corn shrines, the cobalt skies clouded, and a light drizzle
began falling. When the drizzle had eased, the household was in its
nearest garden furiously planting sweet potatoes, yams, beans, and corn.
The Tetum fairly sharply divide labor between the sexes. In planting, the
men give orders while their females and pre-adolescent sons dig the holes
and plant the seeds. As Rubi watched and commented with his six-year-
old daughter (Noko Rubik), Sei Umau, her two sons (Lequi Rubik, aged
15, and Fono Rubik, aged 12) and three of her daughters (Abo Rubik,
aged 17; Cassa Rubik, aged 11; and Siba Rubik, aged 9) seeded the garden. Uncertainty always accompanies the November planting. Should
ceaseless downpours stop a household finishing its work, or if the rains do
not continue during the weeks that follow planting, starvation may await
them. This worry explains why Rubi's household carried out this work in
a somber mood, quite different from their gaiety at harvesting. It is also
the reason why Rubi Loik assisted in the laborious work of planting his
other two gardens. He had a feeling this year's rain would be relentless,
that his family might not get the chance to finish its work. So he bent his
back to the task.

By mid-December, with the corn several feet high, Sei started
gathering green vegetables. Sweet potatoes and yams were also put into
the cooking pot when needed. Corn had to wait until the dry season in
February. After planting, Rubi's family spent most days in their hamlet.
Weeding the three gardens was necessary, certainly, but villagers do not
give this activity undue emphasis, and Rubi was even less concerned than
most. As with the majority of his neighbors, he took advantage of this
break to visit relatives in other hamlets. These had to be local settlements
because the soggy mud of the paths made long trips difficult—another excuse Rubi offered for not attending his growing corn crop. This twelve-
week spell provided him with plenty of opportunity to earn money carv-
ing small buffalo-horn statues for the Administrator, who then sold them
to visiting Australian tourists. Sei weaved cloth which she sold in the Viqueque Village market. Other men specialized in making hoe and spear
blades and other iron implements. Although not as frequent as they
would be during the dry season (June–September), marriages were common. Rubi's family attended several.

46

Left: In the Viqueque Village market a young boy tries to sell dried areca nuts to a woman herself selling corn cobs, bananas and yams.
Below: Ana Soares, wife of Leal, selling lime for betel-chewing. Her customer is filling a bamboo cylinder.

A potter from Macdean village (Uma Kik princedom) placing her damp clay pots beside the fire in which she will shortly bake them. Next day she will take them to the market.

That year the crops were unusually heavy, so the Loiks were in good humor bringing in their harvest. Finishing in four days, they returned home to relax for the last two weeks of February. Rubi had mellowed toward me by now and we cemented our friendship.

March was no more than three days old when under leaden skies the second wet season began. This time, as they made their rounds of the three gardens, Rubi's householders planted dry rice. Females once again performed the grind of labor while their secular superior (Rubi) showered them with suggestions, orders, and what could have passed for encouragement. Work over, they tramped home. The rains were lighter now than in November, December, or January. There were even dry days. With paths firmer, members of the household could spend more time traipsing from hamlet to garden, collecting vegetables, yams, or sweet potatoes and

Having sold her corn cobs and yams, a woman gets up, palm-leaf sack in hand, and prepares to quit the market. In the middle-ground a potter displays her wares.

doing a little weeding. In the first week of April they again planted their gardens with corn and other seeds. From this time on the rainfall became steadily heavier until late in that month when it passed its peak and began to decrease.

By mid-June the rainy season had almost ended. The family was busy weeding, watching in the gardens for marauding birds, picking vegetables and visiting kin. At this time of year I could never be sure of finding Rubi's family, or any other, at home when I called; often I would find Rubi lounging on the veranda of someone else's house in a nearby hamlet while Sei chatted with women friends at the back. July is an excellent month for gathering information. Most families stay in their villages. When they do visit relatives they do not stray far from their hamlets. There is little work to be done, and most people pass the days gossiping or attending marriages. In July of 1967 Rubi Loik was in a jocular mood, but August changed that: the time for work had arrived again.

In August the first job is harvesting the rice. Then the nuts from the family areca trees have to be gathered. Together, these tasks take a week. Then those bachelors who are about to marry raise work-teams from among the fathers' lineage mates. Theoretically, every male should assist his lineage kin when asked. In practice, many ploys are used to evade this duty, and Rubi had been known to exploit most of them. Whatever his past evasions, that August he did lend a hand when a Mamulak man named Funo Lequik wanted a house. Perhaps this was to impress us. By now he knew we had a good idea of the rights and duties kin owe one

Four lads thresh the August rice.

50

another. But if that was his intention, he was only partially successful. Rubi helped some men raise a couple of house poles, split some bamboo for the floor, and harangued the younger men. Then he spent the rest of the time it took to put up the house skeleton drinking and snoozing on a nearby veranda. Nobody troubled him. He would certainly have dredged up some plausible excuse for his sloth, and rather than waste energy lampooning him the other men got on with the job. Rubi occasionally visited his gardens to shoo away birds until early September, when his family harvested their second corn crop. The day after they had taken the corn cobs to the granary in his house, Rubi returned alone to his garden.

September is the month gardens are fired. Men burn the stubble and weeds that have accumulated during the past twelve months, and clear the ground for digging. Rubi Loik went about his job with a will. When he had burned all the rubbish in each garden, he repaired the damage time, rain, and wandering pigs had done to his garden fences. By the time he had finished mid-October had arrived, and the soil needed turning over. His family joined him in the nearest garden. Thrusting their dibbles into the ground, they prised up huge sods and broke the larger ones up; repeating this process in the other gardens. Finally, after a brief respite, they performed the corn ritual. Like the other Caraubalo folk, Rubi Loik's family had negotiated another year.

NATURE AND CULTURE: THE TETUM AND MAKASSAI COMPARED

As a resident of the princedom for such a long time I gradually grew aware that such cultural factors as kinship, acculturation, technology, and history harmonized with the natural factors of topography, soil, and climate. Contemporary society was so much the joint product of both it was impossible to decide which was the more influential. Six of the seven Caraubalo villages are inhabited by the Tetum. These villages and their respective 1966 populations were: Mamulak (375), Mane Hat (496), Vessá (251), Cabira Oan (310), Hás Abut (235) and Lamaclaran (199). The seventh, Sira Lari (160), is the home of people who speak Makassai. In the Viqueque region, the Makassai are mainly an upland folk. The pagan headman of Sira Lari, who bore the wildly inappropriate name João Baptista (John the Baptist), never wearied of extolling the virtues of his highlands. "They have," he used to say, "open spaces, few people, lots of streams, clear water, no mosquitoes, and they are cool." Mamulak knew nothing of these advantages. The village of Sira Lari rests on the northern rim of the Cuha Basin, where the land abruptly rises to the central Timorese massif. It thus provides an ideal case study for the comparative analysis of the different influences culture and nature make on two neighboring peoples who share the same political domain.

Like Mane Hat and Mamulak, the four other Tetum villages are wedged into the basin of the largest river in the area, the Cuha, which flows down from the upland massif to enter the sea twelve miles south of Caraubalo. Near the center of the princedom a belt of hard rock forces the river to veer abruptly westward from its north-south trend before continuing southward to the sea. Inside the loop thus created, an earlier generation founded what is now the Administration settlement of Viqueque Village. Outside this village, hamlets of the six Tetum villages group themselves around both banks. In this central area the soil is more fertile than in the Sira Lari uplands. Gardens and coconut plantations thrive so well here this locality has one of the highest population densities in Timor. Unlike the well-dispersed settlements in the hills, the basin settlements are so concentrated communications are easy, and the proximity of Viqueque Village provides Tetum villagers with greater opportunities than the Makassai to work in Chinese shops or the Administration. Changes have thus been more accelerated here than in Sira Lari. The gently undulating relief of the Cuha Basin, which is part of that river's flood plain, makes it too awkward for extensive irrigation by the Tetum. Of the two wet rice fields owned by inhabitants of the six villages, one belongs to their princedom chief, João da Sá Viana, while the other belongs to the Tuna clan, which has Makassai connections. This fact of ownership is important. One privilege to which João da Sá Viana, as princedom chief, is entitled, is the free labor of up to a hundred Caraubalo villages. So he can afford to maintain such an expensive plot of land as a rice field, and only his household boasts this distinction.

Timorese pigs are mischievous creatures, but they are small enough to be managed by a single youngster in a household and lack the destructive energy of the massive buffaloes. These ungainly creatures cannot be allowed to forage in the Cuha Basin. Even if grazing space existed they would find opportunities to splinter the garden fences and bring lawsuits against their owners. So Tetum villagers rear pigs instead. Some large households do keep a couple of buffaloes because they have six or seven young men to monitor the movements of their beasts. Rubi Loik was an exception. With only two sons he kept a pair of buffaloes and was continually badgered by neighbors complaining of his animals' misdeeds. Outraged gardeners used to pester him for compensation for splintered fences and trampled crops. Toward the end of May, Rubi was missing.

Most days we made a point of stopping at his house, yet three weeks passed before we saw him again. One morning a weary Rubi Loik called upon us with the news that his buffalo cow had gone! He had been searching every inch of the Sira Lari hills to no avail, and was now convinced an enemy had turned her into steaks in retaliation for her smashing fences. We never did learn the truth.

Even for households with a few buffaloes, these beasts are more prestigious than economically important. To be worthwhile, buffaloes must be reared in herds. The herds owned by João da Sá Viana and the Tuna clan could be maintained partly for the same reason that João da Sá Viana and the Tuna people were able to grow wet rice. Abundant human labor was available to them free. Sufficient herdsboys existed to permit grazing on the Makassai uplands. As one party of young men would finish

A small herd of buffaloes untypically encroach on land given over to hamlets. Their size and the relative flimsiness of the houses suggest how easily such beasts can level a hamlet.

its three- or four-day stint it would return home and be replaced by another. The beasts never had to be brought down into the basin.

The Tetum once practiced polygyny, and a wealthy man could have as many as six wives. Occasionally he would marry sisters, and sororal polygyny occurred. With the encroachment of Christianity, polygyny has surrendered to monogamy. The result has been that the typical Tetum household has fewer children than its Makassai equivalent, which, in turn, has reduced the number of potentially free laborers and prevents a household keeping more than a few buffaloes. Had the Tetum lived in the mountains they could have resisted acculturation more stubbornly. The ecological bias toward corn and pigs is a response to both cultural and natural factors.

The interplay of culture and nature also appears in Sira Lari, though here people cultivate wet rice in huge flat or terraced fields and rear herds of two or three hundred animals. João Baptista owned ten buffaloes which formed part of the two hundred-strong herd maintained by his clan. Whereas among the Tetum the largest *effective* agricultural unit is the household, for the Makassai of Sira Lari it is the clan. The number of unpaid workers available to guard the buffaloes and cultivate the rice fields is far larger than is available to the Tetum. The main unit of land exploitation among the Makassai can be much more extensive than is possible for the Tetum, who also suffer the handicap of residing in a heavily populated and physically constricting river basin. The huge work force necessary to build, plant, weed, and harvest either the flat fields or the far

Part of a terraced rice field. Such earthworks require immense labor.

more complex terraced fields can be easily raised by the Sira Lari folk, who in any case have more land. The uplands have plenty of water and the steep gradients make irrigation ditches easy to build and maintain for a large group such as a clan. Difficult communications impeded Makassai acculturation, so today few individuals of this culture are Christians. Polygyny thrives. Households are accordingly larger, and even at this level of group organization the unpaid labor team has more individuals. Herds never lack sufficient youngsters to tend them as they browse on lonely hill tracts or churn up the inundated soil of the rice fields prior to planting the wet rice. These powerful beasts make short shrift of a task which would tax the human resources of even a clan, and the use to which they are put illustrates how intimately wet rice and buffaloes are linked. João Baptista had three wives and nine children, and governed a household of twenty-one persons.

To summarize, then, environmental and social determinants combine to give Makassai ecology its distinctive character. Since these determinants differ from those affecting the Tetum, Tetum ecology is different. On the other hand, their very differences also bring the Sira Lari people and those of the six Tetum villages together. Rubi Loik was self-sufficient in corn and pork—in most years he produced a surplus—but for him rice and buffalo meat were scarce. João Baptista had a surplus of rice and buffalo meat, but lacked corn and pork. So at the market held every Sunday in Viqueque Village the likes of Rubi and João Baptista would trade. Thus were surpluses reduced and demands satisfied.

The House

4

The Caraubalo house, its long body perched on dozens of tiny wooden piles, struck me right away as a remarkable building; but only learning what the Tetum called its different parts and gaining an understanding of the three public rituals (birth, marriage, death) which occur in it made me realize its central value in the local symbolism. Dr. Clark Cunningham's 1964 description of the house symbolism of the Atoni deftly shows how it represents the native cosmos for a Timorese population. For the Caraubalo Tetum, besides symbolizing the dually ordered cosmos it also represents the body of a buffalo and that of a human being. It combines the worlds of the ancestral ghosts and humans, and embodies the complementary contrast between women and men. Although the (secular) abode of the family, it is primarily a (sacred) temple in which communication with ghosts is made. Its symbolic associations incline it toward the feminine elements of the cosmos. In the home wives are definitely the masters.

ARCHITECTURE

The most common house, the one villagers themselves regard as their most characteristic, is the "house with the face." The "face" is the front, and its most striking feature is a wide veranda (Figure 7). Teak piles raise the house three feet above the ground, and pigs, dogs, and chickens grub about under it for most of the day. Unlike the Atoni, the Tetum perform no house-building rites. The prospective house-owner's father assembles the team of housebuilders from his lineage kin and supervises the group. Men chop down trees, shape the trunks and branches, erect the skeleton of the building, thatch the roof, and enclose the sides with bamboo walls. Women bring the dried fronds of the much-exploited palm tree (from which the roof thatch is made) and prepare meals for the workers. If they keep hard at it, two dozen laborers can finish the entire job in ten days. But the team starts losing members after a couple of days and the task force gradually dwindles to less than a quarter of its original size.

Houses are usually about thirty-five feet long, twelve feet wide and fifteen feet high. These measurements include the height taken as the distance from the ground to the gable of the house and the width of the verandas. Three feet of the height includes the teak piles—the "bones which are buried in the earth." The front veranda (the "face") juts out twelve feet from the front door. Extending along one side is a veranda about three feet deep which links the front and rear verandas. The rear veranda is somewhat deeper than the side veranda but not as deep as the front one. All three verandas are supported on piles. Each side wall of the building is called a "leg." Walls and floors are made of split and flattened bamboo. Both the front door and the back door are known as "the steps to the source of life" *(oda matan)*. The term *oda* means "steps," and *matan* means "source," "center," "origin." The term *matan* helps form a large number of longer words. Combined with *u'e* ("water," "center," "source") it becomes *u'e matan*, meaning "well," "spring," or "the Mahuma vagina"; with *ahi* ("fire"), it becomes *ahi matan*, meaning "hearth," "village," or "clan."

The front door is the masculine door. Only men and boys who have attained puberty can pass through it in daily life. Females and younger boys use the rear door, the feminine door known as the house vagina. The front door is called "the eye of the house." In ritual these doors become prominent symbols. The steps descend from the verandas. Each door has one set of steps, and at least one lies along the lateral veranda. They vary in construction—some are stout ladders, others simple bamboo poles tied diagonally to the veranda. The rear steps and door, which together correspond to the *yoni* ("vagina") of Indian sexual imagery, constitute the gateway to the "source of life." The door jambs are called "the fortification of bones;" the rear wall, the "anus." Windows are absent. At sunset each door is blocked with a fan-like screen woven by men from dried strips of fronds from palm trees.

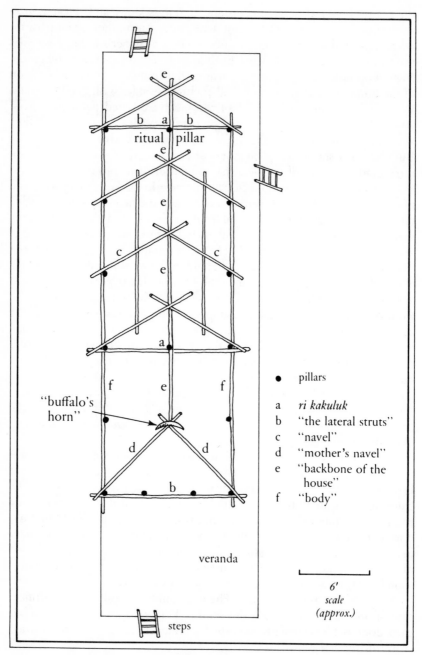

Key within the figure:

●   pillars

a   *ri kakuluk*
b   "the lateral struts"
c   "navel"
d   "mother's navel"
e   "backbone of the house"
f   "body"

Labels in figure: e, b, a, b, ritual pillar, e, e, c, c, e, a, f, e, f, "buffalo's horn", d, d, b, veranda, steps

6'
scale
(approx.)

Figure 7 The skeleton of a Tetum house

58

Top: A Mane Hat house under construction.
Lower: José (right) and a friend perch atop a house skeleton in
Cailulik. This scene is that of a typical hamlet.

At each of the four corners stands a teak pillar twelve feet tall. Five other pairs support the beams and struts (Figure 7) in addition to two central pillars called *ri kakuluk*, one in the rear and one at the front of the building. The rear *ri kakuluk*, or ritual pillar, stands in the same plane as its partner. Around it, runs the ritual shelf. These pillars support "the backbone of the house," the long ridgepole that extends from the back of the house to a point over which the front veranda begins. This ridgepole ends in a curved ironwood support called "the buffalo's horn," and it causes the fronds which provide the roof thatch to overhang the veranda and make it resemble an arbor. The "backbone" is bamboo and fits into the V-shaped notches of the two central pillars, which rise eight feet above the other pillars. As page 59 shows, some houses are strengthened by having two "backbones." One is an upper one (the "elder brother"); its partner is a lower one (the "younger sibling").

The photos also show the pattern of bamboo beams and struts which complete the house skeleton. The sturdiest beams, "the body," run the length of the building on each side. Each connects the front pillars with those at the rear and runs through the side pillars. At right angles to the "body" and connecting three pairs of pillars are "the lateral struts." Slightly longer than the width of the house, they jut from the sides and are tied to the "body" by rope. At intervals along the roof are bamboo struts connected to the "body" at the lower end and to the "backbone" at the upper end; they are known as "the navel." Parallel to the "body" and "backbone" we usually find a long bamboo pole which provides further support for these struts. Sometimes, as in the photos, we find more. Five pairs of durable struts extend up to the "backbone" from most of the pillars. These support the upper section of the building. One pair links the front pillars with the "buffalo's horn." It is "the mother's navel." The veranda lies under it. The thatch is tied to lengths of sago fronds which fall at right angles to the "navel."

The dark interior has three rooms. As we can see from Figure 8, the second largest room has the masculine door. An interior door not in line with the masculine door connects it with the smallest room. No one outside the house can peer inside it, so the privacy of the smallest chamber is preserved. Both together make up the male half of the house, which also includes the front and side verandas.

The largest room is the most important ritually and domestically. It is "the womb of the house" (*uma lolon*), a name which gives us an insight into the symbolic nature of the entire building and fits in with the Tetum notions of birth, creation, and femininity. This room is also "the female half of the house." It includes the rear veranda. The inner door connec-

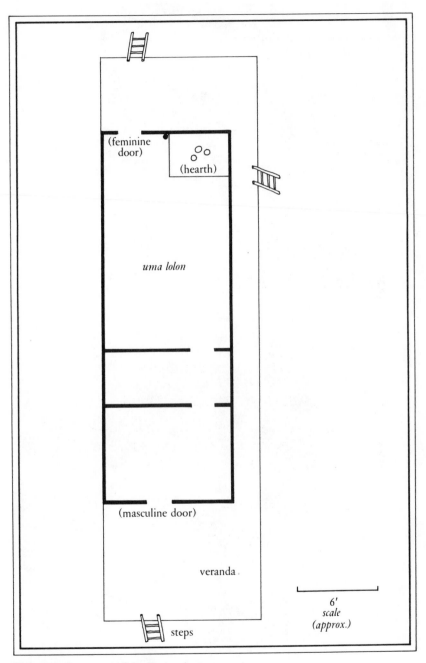

(feminine door)

(hearth)

uma lolon

(masculine door)

veranda

6'
scale
(approx.)

steps

Figure 8 Structure of the Tetum house

Above: Beams, pillars, and struts tied together by dried palm leaves. *Right:* The multi-purpose *tali* palm.

ting this room with the next room is also out of line with the exterior door, but because there is no overhanging arbor a person outside the back door can gaze right into the "womb of the house," a fact which gives point to a couple of lines directed by the prospective bridegroom's father to the bride's mother in Stage 1 of the marriage ritual: "I can see the inside of your garden, the inside of your garden, a flower, a fruit." These are allusions to the womb that produced the girl (the "flower" or "fruit"). The rear wall of the largest room is dominated by the hearth.

The ritual shelf encircles the ritual pillar at a height about four feet from the floor. Lacking decoration and retaining its natural coloring, this shelf is quite ordinary in appearance, and even with its sacred articles gives no hint as to its wealth of ritual value. On the shelf lie the sacred water pitcher *(u'e lolo oan)*, the sacred plate *(hanek matan mutin)* and the sacred cloth *(hena mêan tahan ida)*. From it dangles at least one other article: the pouch of the ancestral ghosts. Every living member of a household owns a sacred pitcher, which as its name ("the little womb") implies, is a small water vessel. It is four inches tall and red in color. Except for the fact that its neck ("vagina") is relatively wider than that of ordinary pitchers, the sacred pitcher resembles a miniature water vessel of the normal type. Pitchers made in the Viqueque region are modeled from clay and sand. Only married women of a village in Uma Kik princedom are allowed to make them.

A pregnant mother purchases a pitcher for her expected child sometime before she is due to give birth, and when its owner eventually dies, his (or her) sacred pitcher is included among those possessions destroyed at the *keta maté* rite which closes the death ritual. Should a pitcher break accidentally, the mother or some other female related to its owner purchases a replacement. Shortly after birth the mother fills the pitcher with cool water taken from one of the larger pitchers standing in the smallest room. When a child of the household leaves the village on a trip lasting more than a month its mother replenishes the sacred pitcher and keeps water in it until he returns. When someone born into the household marries, he (or she) takes the sacred pitcher from the original ritual shelf and places it on the ritual shelf in his new home. Those of the husband and wife are later joined by the sacred pitchers of their children. If the ideal arrangements of post-marital residence and inheritance are fulfilled, a younger son's sacred pitcher remains in the same room from his birth ritual to his death ritual. Villagers say that the pig given to the wife-givers by their wife-takers in the marriage ritual is given "to replace the sacred pitcher the bride brings with her to her husband's house." The sacred pitcher stands for the bride's womb.

A red plate between four and eight inches in diameter, the *hanek matan mutin* ("the plate with a white eye") has a moveable disc *(matan)* three inches in diameter and painted white stuck into its middle. In rituals devoted to Rubi Rika, Lera Tiluk, and Cassa Sonek, and in rites of expiation for moral and social offenses or ritual neglect, betel and food offerings are placed under the disc. Each household has only one of these sacred plates, which a bride purchases soon after she begins residing with her husband. When her daughters marry, the sacred cloth is given to her husband as part of the bridewealth; it is folded under the plate, to remain there until the mother dies. Then it is torn up and discarded. The sacred cloth is folded and put on the plate during Stage 2 of the marriage ritual. When the last surviving spouse dies, the sacred plate is destroyed.

The *hena mêan tahan ida*, "the single piece of red cloth," is a smaller version of the cloth that Tetum men and women wear as a sarong in secular life. Not only do the wife-takers give the sacred cloth to their wife-givers in the marriage ritual, but as we saw in chapter 2, the wife-givers reciprocate with a similar piece of cloth when the offspring of the union are born. In this symbolic context the cloth represents the mother's womb, and it, too, is folded under the sacred plate. The infant is publicly exhibited wrapped in the sacred cloth, and later upon marriage he (or she) takes it to his new home and places it under the sacred plate. At death it is torn into small pieces and cast into the jungle.

The fourth article at the ritual shelf is the pouch of the ancestral ghosts. Each household usually has a single pouch, but some homes whose owners wish to discriminate between the three great princedom ghosts and those of their own clan may have two. At least five houses in Mamulak owned three sacred pouches, the third being the "home" of the husband's third- and fourth-generation ancestors whom he wished to single out for special attention. Normally, one pouch provides a lodging place for all ancestral ghosts. The most frequent visitors are the ghosts of the husband's lineage. In the pouch they rest, sleep, nourish themselves with rice, pork, and buffalo meat, and chew the betel, areca, and lime deposited inside. The pouch itself is an unremarkable bag two inches square plaited by the household head. He does this as soon as he establishes himself in his new house. His wife comes without a bag, and her ancestral ghosts have no contact with her husband's household. The youngest son inherits his deceased father's pouch, which is repaired so often that before many decades are over the pouch is virtually another one. Should ancestral ghosts find that the pouch is empty or in disrepair they make their grievance known by causing sickness.

After a person dies, two pouches are made by members of a group called "the people who give life." One pouch is called "the pouch of the dead," the other "the pouch of the living." The pouch of the dead is placed in the grave. The pouch of the living hangs from the ritual shelf of the dead person's house for exactly one year after the burial before being torn into pieces at the *keta maté* and thrown into the jungle. During this period should the dead soul return to its former home, it is said to notice the pouch of the dead hanging from the shelf, and enter. Finding the ingredients for betel chewing, and rice and pork for eating, it becomes so intent upon consuming these it quite forgets to cause the sickness it had intended. This pouch is physically identical with the pouch of the ancestral ghosts.

SYMBOLISM

Although divided into two sexual and two cosmic halves, the house is more feminine and sacred than masculine and secular. A temple rather than a mere dwelling place, it is appropriate that when the head of a household dies the house is inherited by his *youngest* son, for of a group of brothers it is the youngest who is most closely associated in Tetum thought with the feminine and sacred aspects of the universe. The house is credited with a backbone, eyes, leg, body, anus, face, head, and bones, as well as a womb and vagina, while the presence of a buffalo's horn suggests a visual image of this beast.

These biological similarities and the emphasis on the female sex come together clearly in the following story Agostinha told me on February 3, 1967, in Mane Hat. Often recited at birth rituals, it links the house womb with the human womb, buffalo womb, pregnant stone, and a tree. In some myths, trees seem to belong to that class of object which symbolize the sacred world (recall the two trees at the clan shrine), but the evidence is too contradictory for me to be certain that a connection exists, and so far as I know the villagers themselves do not make it. We should note the reference in this narrative to water pitchers *(lolon)*. The pitcher (especially the sacred pitcher) symbolizes the mother's womb, but unlike the womb itself is not directly used to symbolize the sacred world. Now Agostinha's story.

> Once upon a time a mother buffalo gave birth to a human daughter whom she named Bui Lailua. The girl was a princess. Inside a tree enveloped in dense foliage the mother built their house. One day when the buffalo was out walking human beings searching for food arrived at the house, ransacked it, and took the girl to their village.

On the way they stopped to let their womenfolk scoop water into their pitchers. While the women were doing this a prince came along hunting. As he came near he saw the princess. The prince fell in love with Bui Lailua on the spot, and wanted to marry her. She told him, "You've taken a fancy to me, but watch out! Mother's a wild buffalo." "I'm getting a horse to carry us away," the prince replied. He got the horse, and together they rode off.

Bui Lailua's mother arrived back at the tree to find her only daughter missing. She had gone! The buffalo smelt the girl's trail, sniffed again to make sure, and trundled after her. The runaways reached the top of a nearby hill, looked back and saw the old animal lumbering up towards them. "Bui Lailua," she panted, "why not stop for me?" Her daughter retorted, "Come *on*, mother. I *have* stopped." Then, to the prince, the buffalo cow commanded, "Do the same, my son." But instead of halting the prince took Bui Lailua to his home.

The buffalo eventually reached the prince's house. Inside she could see them "eating" [copulating] in their *uma lolon*. Had she ever caught them! Furious, the buffalo charged at the building, making it buckle. She kept bashing away until its pillars, beams, struts, and verandas were powder. She was so wild that even then she couldn't stop. At the first onslaught the girl had said, "Husband, go and collect every villager who owns a gun. Tell those without to bring their spears." Hearing this, her mother boasted, "No one can wound me. None of this rabble will be able to kill me. All they can do is make me tired. Kill me, they certainly can't. Come home, daughter. I'll kill 'em all. But they won't kill me. What, would you wish me dead? I think I shall become a tree. You still won't be able to kill me. No, you can't. Yes, I'll turn into a 'tree of many fruits.' I shall put down thorny bushes around my tree, so neither pigs nor dogs will be able to nibble at my womb. You'll see. From within the tree I'll make it blossom." The village folk came to help Bui Lailua, but the buffalo's horns slew many. During a lull in the carnage, she took her daughter to one side, showed her "the tree of many fruits," and entered its trunk.

The villagers chopped down the tree and examined it. Just as the old buffalo had predicted, the pigs and dogs could not nibble away at its pith. They returned to their homes. Four days later 'the tree of many fruits' had blossomed. The prince and his wife could see that the trunk had become a pregnant stone, the buffalo's horns were now made of gold, her hide was a magnificent piece of cloth, and her bones made of gold and silver. They carried their treasure home.

The interaction of humans and ghosts, and of male and female, is finely articulated in Tetum house symbolism. As a symbol of the unity-in-diversity of the native cosmos, this temple constantly reminds its inmates of the way their society has chosen to classify the world.

Kin and affines

5

One day in mid-July Maxine and I went to Church. Luís, the eldest son of Miguel da Costa Soares, was marrying a local Chinese girl, and the religious ceremony was being held in the Viqueque Village schoolroom. I mentally noted those persons who attended, making a special point of fixing in my memory the names of the gift-givers.

The next day we visited our friend André, to find out why we had not seen him at the wedding. He was suffering from the effects of a heavy cold, but was as usual pleased to see us. By Tetum standards his was an enormous household. He looked after his quiet, thirty-eight-year old wife, Hílda; two sons, fourteen-year-old José and eight-year old António; two daughters, Rosa (five years) and Domingas (four); and thirteen others, including his widowed mother and his paternal grandfather's brother's son's daughter. Eighteen dependents in all. Most were there that morning, including José.

At once, André wanted to hear our impressions of the wedding. We discussed the persons who had attended and compared the value of their gifts. Then André proudly announced Miguel's son had sent him an invitation, and even more grandly added that because he had been too sick to attend, José, as his eldest son, had for the first time represented him in public and had given André's gift of money to Luís. At this remark José started fidgeting, but I was too engrossed in what his father was saying to sense something was up. Only after I had told André we had not seen his son, and José had begun looking ill-at-ease, did I try to divert the flow of talk into a different channel. Too late! André already had suspicions his wedding gift was not in the right hands. He was right! José quickly confessed he had never got to Viqueque Village, for as he was approaching it he heard the alluring sounds of a cock-fight. The contest was being held a few yards from the road, and he stepped into the jungle "to see whose birds were fighting." Innocent enough. But as José tarried, temptation grew. As I understand it, he was overcome by the entirely altruistic desire to "give a bigger gift to the wedded couple," and there right in front of him was the means of doing so. Fate, alas, was not as charitable. An hour later there was no gift at all, and José was too ashamed to go to the wedding. And now he was trying to talk his way out of trouble. All might

José watching his favorite cocks sparring.

have turned out well—André was getting interested in the details of the cock-fights—but our presence emboldened José (to whom we had just given some wine) and he became casual about his lapse. Seeing his son felt no remorse, André's temperature began to rise, and when José chuckled at some minor piece of abuse André leveled at him, the man lost his temper and cuffed his son's head. Then he seized his shoulder, dragged him into their nearest garden, and made him stay there alone all night. José had failed to honor his duties as a potential member of his father's clan and had publicly insulted his father to boot. Since such conduct invites intervention of the ancestral ghosts in the affairs of their kin, the boy had opened the way for harm to befall his father's clansfolk. To impress this upon his son, André consigned him to the jungle, a place associated with the sacred world. The boy endured that night in terror of a ghostly visitation.

We might think André was unreasonably harsh, but the lesson José had to learn was crucial for any male wishing to assume full adult participation in community life. I said earlier clan membership is conferred by birth, that one is born into a clan. This is literally the case in some societies, but it is not quite as simple as that in Mamulak. Although a baby girl automatically becomes incorporated into her father's clan, her brother acquires only *potential* membership: actual membership is granted or denied when he marries. Of all legal advantages, being a member of a clan is the most useful. Someone outside a clan is considered a non-person in Tetum society. He has no rights and duties; socially speaking, he simply does not exist. And the only clan for which an individual is eligible is that of his father.

Incorporation into a clan occurs when a man marries with bridewealth. Bridewealth is collected from the men of his father's lineage. Men of other lineages are not asked to contribute, nor may they do so even if they wish to. Nor can the bridegroom contribute to his own bridewealth. A typical bachelor would in any case be too young and too poor to contemplate doing so. A man hoping to marry is therefore at the mercy of the senior males whose lineage (and therefore clan) the bachelor hopes to join. They will contribute bridewealth, thereby endorsing the man's proposal for marriage and membership, only if they believe he is likely to prove a worthy member of their descent group, one who will honor his clan and lineage commitments.

When the bachelor's father informs a lineage peer that his son desires the wherewithal to marry, the first thing they discuss is his record since he attained puberty. Has he behaved like a potential agnate? Does he reveal an awareness of their clan's political ambitions? Does he know how its special rituals are carried out? When told to help an older man does he do so willingly or grudgingly? Does he respect his elders? Can he recite his clan's myth of origin? How would prominent ancestral ghosts rate him? This last question is important, for the deceased members of the clan are believed to scrutinize the prospective bridegroom, the bride and her clan, and the manner in which the bachelor's seniors have discharged their responsibility in accepting or denying his application. José would not think seriously of marriage until his early twenties, but he was already adolescent. Whether he fully appreciated it or not he was compiling a credit rating among his kin. Anti-clan behavior, such as André was punishing, would have to be curbed if José were to marry properly and carve a respectable niche in Mamulak social life.

DESCENT

In urban communities of the United States the largest kinship grouping is normally the nuclear (or simple) family. When property is bequeathed the transaction is personal, often (as in the case of wills) with the property passing from a person of an older generation to one of a younger generation. Except for a few restrictions, a person can will his property to anyone he wishes. Wealth does not descend systematically. Some non-literate societies, however, by regulating the passage of property from generation to generation, produce a systematic arrangement. This arrangement we call lineal descent, that is, descent down a traditionally accepted line. One result of this system is that only conventionally specified relatives are entitled to inherit wealth from a deceased relative. The two most widepsread systems of lineal descent are patrilineal and matrilineal. The former brings the father into the line of descent, the second, the mother.

Patrilineal descent (sometimes called patriliny) is a form of lineal descent in which kinship is traced only through males. Females are included in the system, but only insofar as they trace descent through males. Descent groups created by patrilineal descent are called patrilineal descent groups, and we can speak of patri-clans and patri-lineages. Males and females of these descent groups are agnates or kin ("patri-kin" would be more precise). In a patrilineal descent system my father, his brothers and sisters, my brothers and sisters, my children (of both sexes), my brothers' children (of both sexes), and my sons' children (of both sexes) are all included among my kin. Many more relatives could be added to our list, but these would be more distantly related to me. Our list stops at the first ascending generation and the second descending generation. But it could ascend as far as the founders of the clan if we wished to trace descent that far and it could descend to the youngest member of my clan. Among the Tetum this patrilineal descent group owns property in common, and also owns certain political and ritual offices, as well as special rights and duties. Property descends from the men of a higher generation to males of the next descending generation, normally from father to son. In order to keep males of this group together, thus preserving its political strength in the wider community, after marriage brides are taken from the locality where they have lived with their fathers to reside on the property of their husband's clan. This mode of post-marital residence is known as "patrilocal" residence. It is to obtain this privilege (among others) that the groom's lineage gives bridewealth.

Matrilineal descent (or matriliny) is a form of lineal descent in which kinship is traced exclusively through females. As with females in a matrilineal system, males are included in matrilineal groups, but only insofar as they trace descent through females. Descent groups in these systems are known as matrilineal descent groups, and we can talk of matri-clans and matri-lineages. Males and females in such descent groups are kin. The term "agnate" is not used to denote matri-kin, only patri-kin. In a matrilineal descent system my kin include such relatives as my mother, her sisters and brothers, my sisters and brothers, and my sisters' children (of both sexes). Many additional kin could be added to our list if we were to ascend and descend the generations, but persons linked to me by a male link have to be excluded. My father, his brothers and sisters, my brothers' children—even my own children, since I am a male—are therefore outside the range of my kin.

This matrilineal descent group usually owns property in common, and may also own special rights and duties, in addition to certain political and ritual offices. Property descends in the female line, but from *men* of a higher generation to *males* of the next descending generation. Men still manage property and occupy offices even though the link between them is through a female. For instance, inheritance is typically from the mother's brother to his sister's son. Put in a different way, I receive my inheritance from the brother of my mother, and when I die it goes to my sister's son (not to my son, because he belongs not to my descent group but to that of his own mother, my wife). In respect to the senior man, I am his sister's son; in respect to the junior male, I am his mother's brother. Mothers, sisters, and daughters are the key figures in matrilineal systems.

If the matrilineal descent group is to be as effective as possible, it should (like any descent group) keep its members together. But which members? Males or females, or both? The problem is not a mirror opposite of that pertaining in patri-systems. In patrilineal arrangements, females are not essential for the operation of their patrilineal clans; links between males keep the clan together, or rather create it, and members of the male sex run the affairs of the descent group. At marriage, sisters and daughters can be given away completely and reside with their husbands with no loss to their fathers' and brothers' clans. But in matri-systems, although men run their clan's affairs, the clan itself owes its existence not to them, but to their mothers, sisters, and daughters, so that both the males and the females of a matri-clan need to keep together even after their respective marriages. But how can they do this when the prohibition against incest means they must marry *outside* the clan?

Different societies resolve this puzzle differently. One common solution is for the males of a clan to live with their wives' kin after marriage, thus leaving the territory owned by their descent group. Residing with the wife's kin after marriage is called *uxorilocal residence* ("uxor" means "wife"), or sometimes "matrilocal" residence. Because the groom's clan loses his presence and does not gain the presence of his wife, bridewealth does not exist in such systems or is much smaller than in patrilineal systems.

The implications of both types of lineal descent are far-reaching for Mamuluk kinship. Central to their interaction is the institution of bridewealth.

Bridewealth is the collection of gifts the wife-taking group offers the wife-giving group in exchange for a bundle of rights. These rights center on the bride. The first is the groom's right to reside patrilocally, with his father's kin. The second is his right to his bride's sexual and domestic services; these are his exclusively. Much the most important socially is the third right, by which the children of the bride belong to the groom's clan, either from birth or as a result of some later event. Bridewealth, patrilineal descent, and patrilocal residence are parts of the same complex.

Although the Tetum operate a patrilineal descent system, matrilineal descent occasionally appears. All inheritable wealth has to be kept within the clan, though lineages within a clan do have to surrender some property as bridewealth to their various wife-giving lineages. If a man has no sons, his brothers' sons inherit his wealth; if he also has no brother, the sons of the male agnate closest to him in his own generation will inherit from him. A father cannot bequeath anything to a daughter.

Property can be tangible (money, jewelry, pigs, gardens, houses, and so on) or intangible (eligibility for political or ritual office, membership of a social class, and potential membership in a clan). Wealth can also be classed along another axis—secular or sacred. Clothing worn in daily life, weapons in normal use, and eligibility for political office (whether tangibles or intangibles) can be classed as secular property; the Tetum house, ritual clothing, and eligibility for ritual office are types of sacred property. The youngest son inherits his father's sacred property. The other sons inherit their father's secular wealth, with the eldest brother receiving the largest share.

Descent, whether patrilineal or matrilineal, classifies members of a community by assigning them to one clan or another. This gives structure to the society, regulates the transfer of property from one generation to the next, and creates descent groups.

THE MAMULAK DESCENT GROUPS

Figure 9 diagrams the descent groups found in Mamulak, and Figure 10 summarizes their demographies. This village has two clans. The most prestigious, Ina-Aman ("Mother-Father"), is divided into five lineages, which in descending order of prestige are as follows: Ina-Aman, Kia Mahan, Balidi Mahan, Fatuk Mêan Craik, and Nu Laran. (Note that the most prestigious lineage, Ina-Aman, carries the clan name.) Members of this clan trace descent from the three Caraubalo founders, and it owns the territory occupied by Mamulak village. The junior clan, Tuna ("The Eel"), is an immigrant descent group, whose ancestor Léla-sou requested land from the leader of the Ina-Aman folk. Its contemporary members are thus regarded as tenants of Ina-Aman clan and inferior to it. Descending in order of prestige, Tuna clan's three lineages are Bua Laran, Baria Laran, and Cailulik.

Note Mamulak's dual makeup: two clans. Mane Hat, with the two clans of Mane Tolu and Macdean, reproduces it. (The Mane Hat descent groups are shown in Figure 11.) The social organizations of both villages follow the dual track of Tetum thought. Macdean lacks sufficient people to have lineages, but Mane Tolu, a larger descent group, has three. These also are ranked in descending order of prestige: Manecawaik, Maneclaran, and Maneiku. In Mane Hat as in Mamulak, a landlord-tenant association is invoked to determine the status of a clan. Mane Tolu is also considered superior to Macdean because the Mane Tolu ancestors first owned the village land, whereas the ancestors of Macdean were immigrants. We must remember, however, that both villages are peopled exclusively by aristocrats, so this issue of superior-inferior is relative.

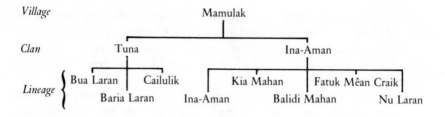

Figure 9 The Mamulak descent groups

Lineage	Hamlets	Households	Population
I. Ina-Aman Clan	2	5	22
Kia Mahan	4	13	60
Balidi Mahan	5	11	43
Fatuk Mêan Craik	6	11	41
Nu Laran	10	21	96
Clan total	27	61	262
II. Tuna Clan			
Bua Laran	1	8	40
Baria Laran	1	4	33
Cailulik	3	9	40
Clan total	5	21	113
Hamlet total	32	82	375

Figure 10 Mamulak Demography. Population of hamlets and households by clan and lineage.

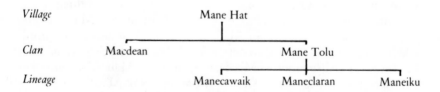

Figure 11 The Mane Hat descent groups

Caraubalo has five other villages. These are inhabited by commoners, members of a social class very much inferior to aristocrats, who remain aristocrats whether descended from landlords or from immigrants. The presence of these contrasting pairs—aristocrats-commoners, landlords-tenants, superiors-inferiors, landlords-immigrants, and dual villages—is typical of the Viqueque region. It is no mere historical accident, but reflects a fundamental pattern of Tetum thought.

The hamlets of Mamulak and Mane Hat are diagramed in Figure 12. According to my informants a lineage should restrict itself to a single hamlet. In reality only Bua Laran (where they had the trouble with ancestral ghosts) and Baria Laran (where André lives) do so. Ina-Aman has two hamlets; Kia Mahan, four; Balidi Mahan, five; Fatuk Mêan Craik, six; Nu Laran, ten; and Cailulik, three. Lineages become dispersed by overpopulation and by quarrels between male kin.

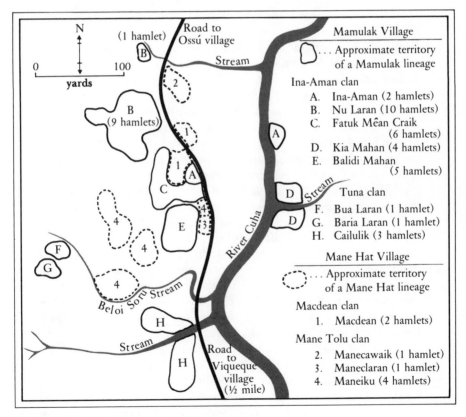

Figure 12   Mamulak and Mane Hat hamlets

Myths justify the claims each clan and its member lineages make for their unique status and exclusive privileges. A person's legal and ritual standing in the princedom and in Mamulak rest entirely upon the place his lineage occupies in his clan and the status of that clan in the village. To repeat a point made earlier, if you have no descent group you have no status in Mamulak; legally, you do not exist. The largest descent group to which a person can belong is the clan, so it is clan membership which makes him an aristocrat or a commoner. Likewise, his chances of playing an important role in Caraubalo and Mamulak are determined by what princedom and village offices his clan owns, not by his own talent or ambition. Ina-Aman clan owns the office of Mamulak village headman *(dato ua'in)*, and within the Ina-Aman clan the Ina-Aman lineage owns this position. No one from the other four Ina-Aman lineages is even eligible for consideration when a Mamulak headman is chosen. Someone from this lineage must be picked, even though as we see from Figure 10, its 1966 population was a mere 22 persons. If it should happen that Ina-Aman lineage could not provide a worthwhile candidate, an able, willing man from another lineage in Ina-Aman clan would be ritually incorporated into Ina-Aman lineage. He would be "reborn" into it, and would assume office as a member of the office-owning lineage. Ritual "rebirth" can be used to fill any office and add to any descent group, so what seems on the face of it a rigid system is really quite flexible. The Mamulak headman's assistant and stand-in, the deputy headman, has to come from Kia Mahan lineage. In Tuna clan, Bua Laran lineage owns the office of secular leader, and Cailulik lineage owns the office of sacred leader. Ina-Aman lineage lacks the office of sacred leader.

When people talk about a clan which happens to be divided into *three* lineages, instead of using the proper names of each lineage (for example, Bua Laran, Baria Laran, and Cailulik) they often refer to them as "eldest brother," "middle brother," and "youngest brother," the relationship terms that would correspond to their secular rank. In Tuna clan these terms are poetic substitutes for the proper lineage names. As we see in Figure 11, in Mane Hat they become the proper names for the three lineages of the Mane Tolu clan. Even though they are poetic substitutes for the Tuna, they give a good idea of the social roles ascribed Bua Laran, Baria Laran, and Cailulik lineages within the clan.

I heard several versions of myths telling how these three lineages came into being. Here is a version that not only describes how Tuna clan came to be created, but also sheds light on the ambiguous status of younger brother in Tetum symbolism. It puts the theme of union-leading-to-creation into literary form, and amounts to a political, historical, and symbolic document. This curious tale was first recited to me in André's house the night of December 26, 1966. It was the first story I collected from the Caraubalo hamlets.

Once upon a time there was an old man called Sorai. He had a wife called Dassarai and seven sons. The youngest was Ali-sou; his nickname was Ali-iku (Ali-the-tail). The eldest was called Léla-sou. One day the seven brothers went traveling in a land known as U'e Klobor. At midday his elder brothers commanded Ali-iku to collect water from a nearby spring. In the spring an eel was making the water muddy. Instead of fetching water, Ali-iku went to tell his brothers. They accused him of lying, and ordered him to return. He obeyed. The water was so dirty he still didn't fetch any. His brothers were derisive, and armed with a chopper Léla-sou accompanied him back. Upon reaching the spring the eldest brother lifted up the eel and hacked it to bits. The two brothers then scooped water into their pitchers and carried the eel back to camp.

His elder brothers ordered Ali-iku to cook the meat in a bamboo tube while they went for a stroll. As it cooked in the tube the eel began speaking! It said:

"*Croto, croto, croto* [the sound of meat cooking]
When the sun sets, Ali-iku
We both shall be eels
We both shall be of the same flesh!"

Astonished, Ali-iku ran to tell his brothers, but by the time they arrived the words had stopped. Again they called him a liar. Their strolling continued. The eel repeated his speech twice, to make a total of three times in all, but Ali-iku's brothers were skeptical. For their meal the other six ate rice and meat that had been fully cooked, but though his rice was well-cooked, Ali-iku's eel meat was still uncooked. At three o'clock all seven washed and frolicked in the spring. When the time came for them to leave, the elder brothers climbed from the water, but Ali-iku couldn't, because while his head was human and he was able to speak his body was like an eel's. He called his brothers to him, saying:

"Well, today I told you what I had seen. Yet you wouldn't believe me. What do you think now? But don't feel sorry for me. Go and buy a red pig and bring it here with some red rice. Then roast the pig and cook the rice." After they had stuffed the meat and rice into a bamboo tube he commanded:

"Put your shares on a plate. Put my share on a banana leaf. On a wide stone covered with a palm leaf place the rice and the meat." This done, they ate. Afterward they listened to his orders;

"Never eat eel!
Neither must your descendants!

Never roast nuts!
Never eat yams!
Never call any of your descendants Léla!
None of your descendants can ever bathe
in the U'e Klobor spring!"

Next he taught them the words of songs and the steps of dances, after which he slammed his head against a rock and this last remnant of his humanity became eel-like, too. The transformation was now total, and the Eel left.

The elder brothers divided up their wealth, their games, and their sacred artifacts. The six split up; three went west, three went east. Of the three who traveled east, one settled in U'e Lako [a village in the nearby princedom of Balarauain], one somewhere else, and one in Uma Fatin [the place where Baria Laran lineage is located]. This last man was Léla-sou. Léla-sou's descendants founded three lineages: Bua Laran, Baria Laran, and Cailulik. Bua Laran owns the clan's wealth; Baria Laran, its games; and Cailulik, its sacred artifacts. These three lineages together make up that clan which we today call Tuna.

Such is the basic version, but there are glosses and additions. On January 3, 1967, in his Cailulik home, Rubi Loik provided one:

Three men traveled eastwards. One stayed in U'e Lako; the other two went further. They asked Ina-Aman clan if they could remain on its land. Members of the clan replied, "If you want to stay here we shall grant you territory." One man kept traveling; the other chose to stay. His name was Léla-sou; and his clan was Tuna.

Agostinha provided a second, on January 21:

When Léla-sou arrived in Caraubalo he asked a favor of the Mane Hat headman and Mamulak headman. These were Rubi Rika and Lera Tiluk. They owned Beloi, which is where the Tuna folk now live. This is the territory Léla-sou eventually received. The two princedom leaders discussed his request. Then they showed Léla-sou four slices of land. They showed him where he could settle down, the territory on which he could build his house and store his possessions. Yes, Léla-sou founded his clan on four tracts of poor land with only lank grasses and infertile soil. But it was still territory worthy of an aristocrat. It was shaped like a huge betel leaf. Léla-sou built his house at a site which later came to be called *uma fatin*, that is, "the place of [Léla-sou's] house."

A typical myth of clan origin, this narrative makes the point that although not the actual founder of the Tuna people (Léla-sou is), Ali-iku really created the clan as a social grouping. By giving it an origin myth, a totem (The Eel), distinctive taboos (the various prohibitions he announced), and songs and dances, he not only civilized it but also distinguished it from all others and was indirectly responsible for Léla-sou (the eldest of the seven brothers) settling down in Mamulak and producing the three lineages into which Tuna clan is divided.

There are three lineages because Léla-sou had three sons. I was told the eldest settled down in Bua Laran after quarreling with his father and brothers, and that the youngest also quarreled and left his father's hamlet to live in Cailulik. Only the middle brother remained in Baria Laran. Hence the present-day geography of the Tuna clan. The relative ages of the three brothers fits their respective statuses and accords with the privileges and duties each brother (and his lineage) was granted in that far-off era. The "wealth" of Tuna refers to its secular property. It includes the Beloi territory, the buffaloes owned by the clan, and the political offices in the village for which Tuna persons are responsible. Bua Laran agnates administer this wealth. The "sacred artifacts" is a symbolic shorthand for "sacred tangible and intangible property," that is, for such ritual paraphernalia as loincloths, the clan shrine, ritual drums, and offices such as the sacred leadership of Tuna clan itself. "Games" refers to the stand-in function of Baria Laran agnates. Their main role in clan affairs is to substitute for members of the secular lineage (Bua Laran) and those of the sacred lineage (Cailulik) at public gatherings if members of these lineages are indisposed. This mediatory role is consistent with their status as the "middle brother lineage."

The two additional texts define Tuna's relationship with Ina-Aman and Mane Tolu (the clan of the Mane Hat Headman). Rubi Loik's version informs us that Léla-sou and his brothers sought permission from Ina-Aman persons only, whereas in Agostinha's version Léla-sou "asked a favor" of the Headmen of both villages. As a Mane Tolu agnate, Agostinha wished to mention Léla-sou's indebtedness to one of her own great ancestors. Nevertheless, both versions make clear that as immigrants and tenants of Ina-Aman, Léla-sou and his descendants were inferior to the already established residents of Caraubalo. Léla-sou gets poorer land.

The tale contrasts the statuses and roles of elder brother and younger brother. If the age difference between two brothers is only a few years, the younger is not considered as inferior as he would be if the difference were greater. A younger brother publicly respects his elder by sitting down to eat at feasts only after his senior is already seated. He must not raise his voice in his elder brother's presence nor strike him. If he is himself a bachelor, he should defer to his elder brother's judgment in political matters. Although usually ignored, these precepts are important enough to be sanctioned by the ancestral ghosts. When a younger brother falls ill the local shaman may lay the blame on some act of filial disrespect. The relationship between elder brother and younger brother resembles that between a man and a woman. Indeed, the Tetum use the same word, *alin*, for "younger brother" and "younger sister." In a situation where there are no females, older brothers order their younger brothers to perform those menial tasks custom assigns to sisters. Ali-iku collects water, cooks food, and serves the meal to his senior brothers just as a woman does for her brothers (elder and younger) or husband. Like women, younger brothers are linked with the sacred world. They inherit the house (or temple), and the "younger brother lineage" of a clan owns its sacred wealth.

As persons associated with the sacred world, younger brothers are as ambiguous in sacred contexts as women. Although the younger brother does not actually assume prominence over elder brothers in ritual, in one area of culture he is given an opportunity to show his dual status as a secular creature and a sacred being. This area is oral literature. In those narratives in which he is the central character, the younger brother is usually involved in some dramatic event which causes his latent sacredness to blossom forth, and by carrying out some fantastic exploit he achieves superiority over his elder brothers. One recurring theme has the younger brother being divested of what little secular wealth he owns by his seniors, and leaving or being banished from his homeland. He often travels across the sea to an unknown land for a while before returning home to astound his brothers with a display of prodigious power, as a result of which he becomes their superior. This foreign land is really the sacred world projected horizontally rather than downward. In his collection of seven Tetum stories, Father Sá (1961) gives three (Texts 3, 4, and 5) which involve the younger brother acting as a mediator between the two worlds. A number of Atoni stories echo the same theme.

Like a woman in ritual, a younger brother in literature occupies a position which in other symbolic situations is occupied by what Turner (1967:110) calls "phenomena...of mid-transition." Straddling both secular and sacred worlds, women and younger brothers are able to use powers denied ordinary inhabitants of both these worlds. They can bring the forces of the sacred world into the secular world to work for the benefit of humans—as happens in the marriage ritual or in the corn rites—and they can take the forces of the secular world into the sacred world to help ghosts and spirits—as occurs when offerings are made. In both cases, women and younger brothers act creatively to bring humans and ghosts together. Ghosts are not invoked in the Tuna myth of origin because that tale describes a time when the clan does not yet exist and therefore lacks ancestral ghosts to call upon. By being transformed into a sacred being, Ali-iku makes their future existence possible because without his strange experience that afternoon by the banks of the U'e Klobor, Tuna clan would never have been created. Tuna agnates have to concede that Rubi Rika, Lera Tiluk, and Cassa Sonek are the most eminent of all ghosts because they belong to clans more prestigious than their own, but they have a special fondness for their first ancestral ghost, Léla-sou.

EXOGAMY

Each of the two social classes, aristocratic and commoner, is *endogamous*. In other words, aristocrats cannot marry commoners, and commoners cannot marry aristocrats. But descent groups in all lineal systems are *exogamous,* and intermarry. One distinction often drawn between clans and lineages is that whereas clans are exogamous only in theory, lineages are exogamous in practice. In Mamulak this distinction holds up quite well, though I know of several instances of kin from the same lineage marrying one another. Although not a descent group, the hamlet is the largest grouping that maintains its exogamy. Each lineage within the same clan traces its founder to the sixth generation. At the seventh is the clan ancestor. For the Tetum the number seven, like the number three, signifies the idea of unity. This is why the clan's *apical ancestor*, that is, the one at the very top of the family tree, is always spoken of as having lived seven generations ago. Strange as it might seem to us, both José and André used to tell me that Léla-sou was seven generations removed from them—although father and son belonged to different generations! The three sons of Léla-sou are said to be six generations removed from these two contemporary members of Tuna clan. As in so many patrilineal and matrilineal systems, historical and biological facts take a poor second place to political and religious expedience.

COOPERATION AND CONFLICT

The strongest and most varied rights and duties are those binding a male or female to his or her household. Outside this unit their strength depends upon kinship distance, occasion and personality. A man from one of the three Cailulik hamlets, for example, would not expect a clansman in Bua

Laran or Baria Laran to help him as readily as he would an agnate from Cailulik lineage, and assistance would come more speedily from a resident of his own hamlet than from a kinsman in one of the other Cailulik hamlets. This is "kinship distance." No one outside your own lineage is obliged to help you build a house or garden, or to raise bridewealth for your son; but if you are arraigned before the village court by a person from another clan, every kinsman in your own *clan* must back you. However, should you be respected as a clansman who promptly assists even distant kin, when you need help you will most likely find that even persons under no legal constraint to help you will do so. And if you have helped affines they may reciprocate.

Most quarrels erupt between kinsmen who live near one another and who work together. Disputes arise between women and between affines or non-related persons, but most conflicts and their degree of intensity follow the contours of kinship distance, occasion, and personality. They are the reverse side of rights and duties. Conflicts between older unmarried brothers sharing their father's household are the most common. As we might guess from the treatment meted out by André to José, the father-son relationship is also fraught with strong undertows of hostility. Spiteful quarrels develop when an agnate who considers himself entitled to help is refused. Excuses are legion, and even legal obligations can be plausibly evaded. The closer the kinship distance and the less the geographical space between agnates, the greater the danger physical violence will break out. Every clansperson nevertheless realizes full well that his social existence depends upon maintaining working kinship contacts. Ancestral ghosts are swift to punish evaders of agnatic duties or those who keep up festering relations with kin. Conflicts are thus resolved one way or another, usually by an elder mediating between the two parties. If the issue remains unresolved, personal relationships between them will deteriorate until one or both leave their hamlets to set up new homes elsewhere.

Of all the occasions for cooperation and conflict, the most highly charged emotionally is that which occurs when lineage agnates are asked for contributions toward the bridewealth of a kinsman's son.

BRIDEWEALTH

In most marriages it is the lineage which acts as the alliance group, that is, the descent group which raises the bridewealth in its wife-taking role, and disperses the bridewealth among its members in its wife-giving role.

Since at any particular moment men of a lineage will be in the process of marrying women from several other lineages while their female agnates will be marrying men from several other lineages, a lineage will often be simultaneously wife-giver and wife-taker to a number of other lineages.

Although marriage can establish a young man as a full-fledged member of his father's clan and is of crucial affinal value in Mamulak society, the native language surprisingly has no single word which even approximates our general term "marriage." The Mamulak people, however, do have specific names for their two most important types of marriage: the *hafoli* and the *habani*.

The typical Mamulak marriage is the *hafoli*. This is defined by a system of descent that is patrilineal, a post-marital residence that is patrilocal, firm affinal commitments between the two affinal lineages concerned, and bridewealth. The *habani*, while common enough, is regarded by the villagers as untypical of their kinship system. In it, no bridewealth is given, nor are any affinal ties formed between the groom's lineage and that of his bride (in fact, the groom has no lineage). It is defined by a system of matrilineal descent for the offspring of the union and uxorilocal residence for the groom. Both types of marriage illustrate the general features of lineal descent, post-marital residence, and bridewealth, discussed earlier.

The term *hafoli* means "to make up the bridewealth." The bridewealth consists of two kinds of gift: the symbolic bridewealth and the economic bridewealth. The gifts (comprising the symbolic bridewealth) are collectively known as the *na'an tolu*. The economic gifts are called by the same term as the entire bridewealth (both symbolic and economic), namely, *folin*. The symbolic bridewealth itself is made up of two parts: the *na'an* ("the meat") and the *modok* ("the green vegetables"). The *na'an* part consists of a buffalo, a horse, a pig, and fifty *patacas*. A *pataca* is an old Mexican coin brought to Timor by the Portuguese. It no longer circulates. *Patacas* are included among the sacred artifacts of a clan. In the bridewealth, the fifty *patacas* are known as the *pataca lima nulu*. The *modok* is made up of five *patacas* and a sacred cloth *(hena mêan tahan ida)*. No *hafoli* can take place without "the meat," but if the two lineages are of about the same social prestige and the marriage is as attractive to the wife-givers as it is to the wife-takers, "the green vegetables" can be omitted. The amount of money and the quantity and quality of the animals offered the wife-givers in the economic bridewealth depend upon the relative statuses of the two groups.

As in many lineal descent systems the social implications of marriage far outweigh personal considerations. The *hafoli*'s main intention is to bring two lineages into a relationship; or, if previous marriages already bind them together, to maintain that relationship. If a young man is granted bridewealth by his father's lineage, his father collects it from the senior men and eventually sees to it that it is delivered to the father-in-law, who later distributes it among senior male agnates of his own lineage. If a prospective groom fails to obtain bridewealth, he has one of two options available: postpone marriage, in the hope that an improvement in his behavior may change his father's agnates' estimation of his agnatic potential; or go ahead with his plans and marry in a *habani* union. If he elects the second course, the young man relinquishes all prospects of becoming *anyone's* kinsman.

By marrying in the *habani*, a groom "makes himself a father-in-law"; that is, apart from his wife, he creates his father-in-law as the most influential person in his life. But he lacks kin. The senior man's influence is partly a function of the son-in-law's uxorilocal residence. Until his wife has given birth the young man must actually reside as a dependent in his father-in-law's house. Once he becomes a father himself, the young man is permitted his own house, but must still reside in the father-in-law's hamlet. Although he obtains control over his wife's sexual favors, the groom is obliged to share her domestic services with her father, her unmarried brothers, and her mother. Lacking any standing in his wife's lineage, an uxorilocally residing husband finds himself abjectly inferior to his father-in-law's male agnates. The adult members of this group have authority to compel his help in such activities as house-building and gardening. They owe him nothing. A son-in-law can never hold office in any clan, and his children and their descendants inherit the stigma of tracing descent through a female (his wife). Belonging from birth (if they are girls) or potentially (if they are boys) to the clan of their mother's brother, the children of such a marriage trace descent matrilineally. They are members (actual or potential) of a matri-clan, not of a patri-clan.

Marriage is important because it determines which Mamulak rules of descent, post-marital residence, and affinity are called into operation. The *habani*, lacking affinal consequences, also lacks ritual accretions. Ritual, on the other hand, turns the *hafoli* marriage into a public event of note, as we shall see in the next chapter.

Marriage

6

Three related acts of union in the marriage ritual express the theme union-leading-to-creation. Each creates its own special product. Bridegroom and bride unite to create a new human being. Wife-takers and wife-givers unite to create mutual ritual benefits. Humans and ghosts unite to ensure these two unions are fertile and to help ghosts live comfortably in the other world. We saw that in the birth ritual the wife-givers represent the secular, masculine world of human beings whereas the wife-takers symbolize the sacred, feminine world of the ancestral ghosts. This association reverses itself in the *hafoli* ritual.

Villagers in their poetic imagery refer to the *hafoli* as "the spoon and the plate." This homely image suggests the ritual, sexual, and cosmic interdependence of these three paired contrasts (bride and groom, wife-givers and wife-takers, ghosts and humans). The contrasts in each pair are like the spoon and plate. They are essential for a meal to be eaten. (Recall here the equation between copulation and eating in the Bui Lailua tale.) In the symbolism of many cultures the two acts are classed as identical in certain contexts. In many languages "to eat" and "to copulate" are the same verb. In the phrase "the spoon and the plate" additional symbolic innuendoes enrich its primary meaning.

THE STAGES OF THE RITUAL

After the elders of the two lineages have agreed to the marriage, a *hafoli* can begin in one of three ways. In that variety known as the *hussu feto* ("to surrender the bride") the two lineages agree to the details of the bridewealth, which is then handed over during the next eighteen months or less according to circumstances. Villagers consider this the most satisfying of all variations of marriage. Statistically, it is by far the most common. The next most frequent is the *sai tan feto*, "the girl who leaves her father's house to become a mother," which occurs if the girl is pregnant. Marriage by no means invariably follows the discovery that a spinster is with child. If the lovers do not want to marry or if their descent groups are unwilling to arrange the match, the marriage cannot take place. The children of unmarried women are not bastards. Illegitimacy is unknown. Children born out of wedlock become the legal children of their mothers' fathers or mothers' brothers. If their mother later marries, they are then adopted by her husband. Unless she has had a whole brood of children, no stigma attaches to a spinster. Nevertheless, if she marries in a *hafoli*, the groom himself, and not his father, visits his future father-in-law's house to formally request permission to marry the girl. The third variety is that in which the suitor comes to his sweetheart's home and elopes with her to his own father's house. Its title is the *foti feto* ("to carry off the bride"). The *foti feto* comes about if the wife-takers anticipate difficulties in raising even the initial gifts which make up the bridewealth. The elopement saves face for them, and when the total bridewealth is finally paid off they must add a pig to the symbolic bridewealth "to lower the anger" of the girl's father.

Four stages mark the progression of the *hussu feto*. The *sai tan feto* and the *foti feto* have three. These are stages 2 through 4 in the following description.

Stage 1

After deciding to marry, the lovers sound out their parents. If the parents are sympathetic, the two fathers informally chat about the possibilities with senior males of their respective lineages to discover whether any serious political or kinship impediments exist. If no problems appear, and the marriage is to be a *hussu feto*, the groom's father pays a formal visit to his future daughter-in-law's house to begin the *hafoli* ritual. His visit usually comes about a week after the lovers first make their wishes known. When the father arrives at the house he calls out to the girl's mother to come to the top of the steps at the entrance to her house vagina. Since this is a sacred ritual, the woman, who is to become the priestess of the *hafoli* ritual, is superior to the man. Accordingly, she stands at the top of the steps while he remains at the bottom. From below he can peer into the dark depths of the house womb, and as he gazes up at the mother he says:

"I can see the inside of your garden   1
The inside of your garden
A flower
A fruit
My eyes wish   5
My son desires
That I come to talk to you
That I come to persuade you."

She replies:

"How many flowers?   1
Six coconut palms?
How many fruits?
Six coconuts?
Perhaps something like an orange   5
Get hold of something like an orange
Find a length of cord
Carry the oranges tied up
Look for the ring
Come with the ritual words   10
Tie a cord
An orange
An orange
Make your agnates go, go
Come, come   15
Let them see
Let them see
An orange
A prohibited orange
A prohibited one."   20

In unison they both say:

"A mother has two breasts   1
A father has two breasts
The eye wants the cord
The mind desires a cord

Search as though you go to   5
Fetch water for cooking meat
Collect firewood to cook the meat
Bind we two together with cord
My daughter can then depart
The mat goes   10
Apply yourselves without sleeping
Stir your lineage into action
Hurry your lineage."

The father then leaves.

The ring is a special noose an owner attaches to an object he wants
to stamp as his property. Line 9 of the mother's speech urges the father to
find one so he can signal his son's claim on the bride. This is a reference to
the symbolic bridewealth *(na'an tolu)*. Since the gifts making up this
collection of bridewealth are given to the father-in-law they usually assert
the groom's claim. The "fruit" and "flower" of the mother's womb (in
the first four lines of the opening speech) are the bride herself. As the
father looks into the womb of the house in which the girl was conceived
and born (and from which she emerged through the house vagina in the
birth ritual) he is, as it were, peering into the "inside of the mother's garden." One image formed here is of the household gardens, the "fruits"
and "flowers" of which the mother has cultivated. The mother's
questions in the second speech (lines 1 through 4), beginning with "How
many flowers?" are ways of asking the size of the economic bridewealth.
There will later be much horse-trading over this matter, and in language
far from poetic. The "orange" symbolizes the symbolic bridewealth; two
items—the ring and the cord—symbolize the link being created between
bride and groom, wife-givers and wife-takers and ghosts and humans.
Once part of the "orange" gift has been given the bride is "prohibited" to
other males (second speech, lines 16–20). In the third speech (lines 3–4),
the cord symbolizes the horse (one of the bridewealth items). The
mother's command to make the male kin "go" and "come" (second
speech, lines 14–15) evokes and image of the wife-takers scurrying to and
fro between their hamlets delivering the bridewealth. In the third speech,
the "mat" (line 10) which "goes" is the mat upon which the groom and
bride sit in Stage 2. It "goes" with the bride when she departs for her
husband's house. The command in line 8 to "Bind we two together" ad-
mirably fits the unifying theme of the ritual, and images of union twine
their way through both the second and third speeches. The "two breasts"
denote the intimacy of the bonds between mother and daughter and
between father and son.

From now on the father-in-law is called "the backbone and corners of the house, the hearth stones and fireplace of the house." The father-in-law has this title because it is in his house the main part of the ritual is enacted.

Before the next stage begins the groom visits his father-in-law at least twice. Each time he gives the senior man a suckling pig or a small quantity of money as tokens of respect. On his first visit a bachelor offers a gift which carries the name "to knock on the door," i.e., the door which opens into the vagina of the father-in-law's house. Here lies the source or origin of his future children. The present given on the second visit is "the cord of possession." This phrase refers to the affianced status of the girl. By accepting the second gift and uttering the following three lines of ritual verse the father-in-law personally betroths his daughter to her suitor, establishing the first symbolic link between their respective lineages. The symbolic bridewealth is the tangible expression of the affinal link between these two descent groups. The "cord of possession" represents the link between father-in-law and son-in-law. The father replies:

> "Bean tree and fruit tree
> Carve an alliance between our two lineages
> Establish an alliance between us."

When cut, the barks of the bean and fruit trees exude a reddish secretion. The two trees symbolize the two lineages; the secretion itself symbolizes blood, the blood which carries the life of each lineage from one generation to the next. The bloodstream of both groups will unite completely in the baby, the product of the marriage. Blood itself also symbolizes the idea of union, so a double symbolism is created.

Stage 2

The *sai tan feto* and *foti feto* begin with this stage, and from here on are identical with the *hussu feto*. This stage ideally takes place a month after the father's visit to the girl's mother. If the gifts cannot be collected in that time, Stage 2 is delayed until they are ready. Once the bridewealth has been gathered it is delivered in two parts (note how often the number two occurs in the symbolism) to the bride's father. The first part is given in this stage.

Stage 2 has a title: "to go in order to reach an agreement." Three of the six items making up the symbolic bridewealth are given in this stage: the pig, the five *patacas*, and the sacred cloth. Collectively, they are called: "the bargain to be struck in the father-in-law's house, the untying of his

With their backs to the camera, Funo Loik's wife-takers discuss bridewealth with their wife-givers in Stage 2 of the marriage ritual. This occurred in July 1967.

door." Giving these entitles the wife-takers to enter the womb of the father-in-law's house to discuss the size of the economic bridewealth and the length of time for payment.

The *patacas* and sacred cloth lack poetic names. The pig is called the *sidi dua, beti dua; hanek matan mutin, u'e lolo oan.* The *hanek matan mutin* is the sacred plate. The *u'e lolo oan* is the sacred pitcher. Villagers translated *sidi dua, beti dua* for me as "like two strangers meeting." They said the entire expression denoted the union of the bride with the groom, the wife-givers with the wife-takers, and the ghosts with humans.

Every man in the wife-taking lineage may attend the Stage 2 proceedings, and the senior men of each hamlet in the lineage must attend. The groom and his father both take part. Should the marriage involve a Mamulak person and one from Mane Hat, the Mamulak headman and the Mane Hat headman (or their representatives) are expected to appear, at least for a few minutes. Most elders of the two lineages do usually turn up, together, with the groom, the bride, their parents and first degree kin, and about half a dozen younger male agnates. Women from the wife-taking group are officially discouraged from attending, but a few always appeared at every marriage I attended. Wife-giving females can attend, a privilege arising from the feminine-sacred associations of their group.

Two young bachelors representing the wife-takers and two representing the wife-givers open the proceedings on the appointed day, after the wife-taking pair have led their kin into the father-in-law's hamlet. They are greeted by the wife-giving pair, the senior of which accepts the three gifts. To emphasize their association with the sacred world the wife-taking bachelors address the wife-giving bachelors as "ancestors." The wife-taking bachelors carry the gifts into the womb of the bride's house, placing the coins and cloth on the ritual shelf and the pig (whose fore and rear legs are tied together) on the floor between the hearth and the ritual pillar. Then they escort their elder agnates to the house womb while the wife-takers and younger members of the wife-giving lineage stand in the plaza of the hamlet. After the bride's kin have

Baskets upon which pouches containing areca, betel and small bamboo cylinders holding lime are placed before being offered to guests at birth, marriage and death rituals. Note pouch in basket on right.

settled themselves near the pillar the wife-taking bachelors lead their agnates into the womb, where they sit near the walls. On a mat between her kin and the pillar sits the bride. Standing nearby is the priestess, her mother. The fiancé is the last person to enter the womb, which is so jammed with people he always has to shove his way to the mat on which his bride is sitting. He takes his place beside her. On this mat, which the bride will take to her new home, they will eventually copulate, and on it she will give birth to the offspring of their union. The priestess picks up the sacred cloth, drops the five *patacas* in the sacred plate, folds the cloth and covers the plate with it. After putting seven betel leaves, seven areca nuts, and a small pouch containing lime on the sacred cloth, she sits down between the groom and bride. To her left is the man; to her right, the woman. With betel, areca, and lime in special pouches hanging from their waists, the wife-taking bachelors offer these ingredients for chewing to their hosts. Their counterparts do likewise for the wife-takers, extracting the betel, areca, and lime from a voluminous sack at the foot of the pillar. When all but the three on the mat have begun chewing, the priestess rises and goes to the ritual shelf. From it she takes three betel leaves, three areca nuts, and a little lime. These she holds in her left hand. She takes the same quantity in her right hand, bends over and gives the man the contents of her left hand and the girl the contents of her right. As they start chewing she helps herself to a single leaf, a nut, and some lime. Sitting down between the youngsters, she, too, begins chewing.

The seating arrangement underscores the separateness of the two affinal groups, but once the ritual has made this point it then asserts the interdependence of the two lineages. The wife-takers must rely upon their wife-givers for their supply of betel-chewing ingredients; the wife-givers must rely upon their wife-takers. Here, *union follows separation.* The wife-givers' superiority explains why they receive the ingredients before their affines and why they sit nearer the ritual pillar. The symbolism of the groom and bride also suggests unity and separation. Sitting together, or uniting, on the same mat on which they will soon sleep and copulate, they are then separated by having different sets of betel-chew. Since the groom is a wife-taker and the bride is a wife-giver, the priestess not only acts as mediator between male and female, she also mediates between the two lineages. Later, in praying, she directly brings together humans and ghosts. The marriage ritual emphasizes the idea of union more strongly than that of separation. Separation merely sets the scene by asserting the distinction that exists between the opposites. Hence the presence of those two Tetum symbols of union, the numbers three and seven; three recurring generally in the number of leaves and nuts and in the number of persons sitting on the mat, seven occurring specifically in the number of leaves and nuts placed on the sacred cloth.

To acknowledge the drama's major theme, just as the priestess begins praying, the groom and bride exchange the two sodden masses of betel and nut they are chewing. He chews hers and she chews his.

On the mat the girl holds the priestess' right hand in her left hand and the priestess holds the man's right in her left hand. When the priestess gives the betel, areca, and lime to the couple she puts the groom's portion in his right hand and the bride's portion in her left hand. As mediator, the priestess is both secular and sacred. Insofar as she is secular, when she makes contact with the ancestral ghosts or the girl (who as a female is sacred) the priestess reveals herself as being of the masculine, secular world. Hence she offers the bride her right hand. Standing as she does for the sacred, feminine world, the girl herself extends her left hand. The hand symbolizes the sexual and cosmic nature of its owner, so the masculine, secular groom grasps the priestess's left hand in his right. From his point of view she, as a woman, stands for femininity and sacredness.

The prayers uttered by the priestess confirm the theme of union-leading-to-creation. The references to "breath" and "blow" evoke a mental picture of ancestral ghosts infusing fertility into the bodies of the couple. Their fertile bodies are likened to the fertile soil. The following speech and the speeches of the bachelors in Stage 3 I have translated and adapted from Duarte's exceptionally rich 1964 original and included verses I recorded myself.

The priestess says:

"I blow on these betel leaves	1
I blow on these areca nuts	
Before putting them into your mouths	
Woman and man	
So our ancestral ghosts will breathe into your bodies	5
So their breath may penetrate your bodies	
So your bodies may be healthy	
So your bodies may be well	
Like good earth	
Like good mud	10
So you may have as many offspring as betel	
So you may bear fruit like areca	
Creating many leaves	
Producing many fruits	
Fertilizing rice fields	15

Fertilizing rice terraces
Replenishing our princedom
Replenishing our *u'e matan*
Multiplying yourselves in our princedom
Multiplying yourselves in our *u'e matan.*"   20

The groom and bride accept the ingredients for chewing from the left and right hands respectively of the priestess. Sitting down, the priestess intones:

"Both of you have received these betel leaves
Both have taken these areca nuts
Therefore, may our traditions and rules as well as the breath
Penetrate your bodies
May they remain forever in your bodies."

The groom and bride exchange betel spittle, and for the third time the priestess addresses the couple:

"Today   1
Now
Our two lineages
Our two descent groups
Like two branches, unite   5
Like two branches, unite
You two persons interlock
You two individuals interpenetrate
Your two bodies shall become as one
Your two bodies shall become as one   10
We old women and old men
In teaching you
In leading you
Into the middle of the garden
Up to the foot of the wine tree   15
Will teach you our traditions
Will teach you our rules
You two
Woman and man
When you walk reflect upon this knowledge   20
When you sit down remember it
We, old women and old men
Taught you it with our lips
Instructed you with our words

94

You both are already a single body   25
Two persons, but one body
We are entrusting secular authority to you
We are entrusting sacred authority to you
Yes, into the hands of you both
So that you may govern your household jointly   30
May this dual authority unite you
You, man, when you awake in the morning
Don't neglect your duties
When you sit down
Remember them   35
Don't forget them when you eat
Don't ignore them when you drink
Remind yourself of your duties when you work
Remember them when you play
Recall them by night as well as by day   40
Obey their demands
When tempted to ignore your duty, resist!
You, woman, attend to your duties likewise
Obey your husband in secular matters
Follow his advice in secular matters   45
In things small
In things big
Both of you will get your just desserts
The ghosts will see you receive what you earn
Share a single sleeping mat   50
Share one pillow
You are as united as the spoon and the plate
You cohabit in the same house womb
You live under the same roof
Husband, don't think of another woman   55
Wife, don't think of another man
If you quarrel
If you, wife and husband, shout at each other
Do not call upon your lineages
Don't seek support among your hamlets   60
You must resolve the argument by yourselves
As best you can
Protect each other's interests
Do good to each other
Protect the interests of each other's kin   65

Protect the interests of your own kin
Help them in secular matters
Help them in sacred matters
So the ancestral ghosts
Will not punish you   70
So your bodies will not fall ill
May your bodies remain healthy
May your bodies remain healthy
Like your sacred pitchers
Like your sacred plate   75
Like a wholesome banana
Like a stick of sugar cane
Like good earth
Like good mud
So you may have as many offspring as betel   80
So you may bear fruit like areca
Creating many leaves
Producing many fruits
Fertilizing rice fields
Fertilizing rice terraces   85
Replenishing our princedom
Replenishing our *u'e matan*
Multiplying yourselves in our princedom
Multiplying yourselves in our *u'e matan.*"

The priestess then stands up and takes a position near the ritual shelf.
Removing the betel-spittle from her mouth, she puts some under the
sacred cloth and the remainder into the sacred plate. She prays *sotto voce*
to the ancestral ghosts. She asks them to confirm all she has said, make
the marriage fruitful, ensure that the two lineages gain bountifully from
their partnership, and help their own relationship with their human kin to
be mutually profitable.

Most persons inside the house now go home, but the senior men of
both lineages reassemble on the veranda, the wife-givers sitting near the
wall of the house and their affines sitting at the veranda's edge. Women
serve rice and wine, as the men haggle over the size of the bridewealth
and argue about how it is to be paid. When at last night threatens to draw
its cloak over them the wife-takers and those wife-givers from other
hamlets leave. If no agreement has been reached, the meeting reconvenes
the following morning, and the affines keep meeting until a bargain has

been struck. Then, the wife-takers set about raising this economic part of the bridewealth.

The four bachelors meanwhile visit the house of the Caraubalo chief, João da Sá Viana, in Viqueque Village to invite him to Stage 4. The bride is now free to live in her husband's house or, since his own house is probably still being built, that of his father. She is now a married woman.

Stage 3

Although poorer lineages may take over a year to raise all the bridewealth they owe, most lineages only take about a week to implement the agreement reached with their wife-givers. The wife-givers want to get their hands on the presents as soon as possible, so this stage often begins even though only a few items have been accumulated. The remaining items are given in Stage 4. In rare circumstances they may even be postponed beyond that. In practice, stages can overlap. But during Stage 3 the other three items making up the symbolic bridewealth (the horse, the buffalo, and the fifty *patacas*,) are expected to be delivered to the father-in-law, and at least half of the economic bridewealth. Of this stage villagers say:

> "Relying on each other's honesty   1
> Accepting each other's word
> Cautiously
> The word of the wife-takers
> The word of the wife-givers."   5

On the day of the meeting the wife-taking bachelors escort their kin to the father-in-law's hamlet. There they are at once met by the other pair and their agnates. The wife-taking pair returns to the theme of union-leading-to-creation:

> "Again we looked for the bean tree and fruit tree
> We carry a knife to make an alliance
> We carry a knife to carve an alliance."

An agnate chosen by the father-in-law steps forward to inspect the beasts held by the wife-taking bachelors. Should any fall below his standards the man rages at his guests, telling them to take their miserable gifts and go. Then, stalking furiously to the father-in-law, who has meanwhile been squatting in his house, he gives him his evaluation as the wife-takers stand about muttering defensively. The inspector emerges from the house through the male door, glances scornfully toward them and immediately re-enters. His silence confirms the father-in-law's rejection. In principle, the father-in-law can ignore his agent's opinion and accept the animals, though I never saw this happen. If he accepted bridewealth condemned by his own man, the father-in-law's prestige would decline. The next time, better quality livestock is offered, and if he judges them inadequate a second time the inspector again rails against the wife-takers. When he considers the gifts good enough, the agent orders the wife-giving bachelors to fetch the father-in-law from his house. After seeing the beasts the man usually ratifies his inspector's verdict. But not always. One afternoon in July 1967 Funo Loik of Maneclaran lineage in Mane Hat derided the groom, a pleasant young lad from Bua Laran, and demanded better animals. As Maxine and I looked on, his senior kin tried vainly to persuade him to accept his agent's judgment, but by sheer nastiness the disgruntled man got replacements.

The animals accepted and the father-in-law's thanks conveyed to the wife-takers, the priestess emerges from the house womb to conduct the senior elders of both lineages into the house. They sit down as before. The room is emptier now, and the congregation remains only a few minutes. Facing the ritual shelf, the priestess takes some lime plus a single betel leaf and an areca nut from the seven she has earlier placed on the sacred cloth, and chews. When the mixture is red enough, the priestess with her right hand takes the mass from her mouth and slips it onto the sacred plate. This is an offering to the ancestral ghosts who are asked to confer those benefits requested in Stage 2. She then invites everyone to follow her through the house vagina and into a building temporarily constructed in the hamlet. This done, her priestly role ends.

Wife-givers build this temporary house a few days before the meeting; it is a flimsy thing, rarely lasting more than a couple of seasons. In each pair of bachelors the older acts as speaker. The two seniors (WT1 and WG1 in Figure 13) sit facing each other. When the men of the two lineages have settled themselves down on the elevated floor of the building, women from the host group mount the steps leading to the floor and distribute the ingredients for betel-chewing. These they offer first to their guests, and then to their own kin. The two senior bachelors accept their betel-chew, but chew only after they have finished their respective speeches. As soon as everyone else is chewing and the gay chatter which began while the spectators were filling the building settles into an expectant hush, the senior wife-taking bachelor is ready to speak.

If he fluffs a few lines here and there his kin prompt him. Members

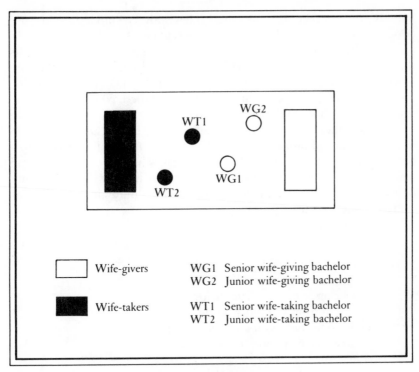

Wife-givers   WG1   Senior wife-giving bachelor
                          WG2   Junior wife-giving bachelor

Wife-takers   WT1   Senior wife-taking bachelor
                          WT2   Junior wife-taking bachelor

Figure 13   Seating at the marriage ritual, stage 3

of the wife-giving group may also interject help, but if it becomes clear the bachelor has not bothered to learn his lines the wife-givers are authorized to levy a fine on his group. This fine is a pig. It is called the "fault," and it becomes the father-in-law's property—"to hide his shame." If the previous bridewealth discussions were carried out with good will and an agreement speedily reached, the fine is normally waived. But if the bargain was struck in an atmosphere of hostility, or if some of the proffered livestock had to be replaced, the wife-givers always demand the pig. (Funo Loik certainly made this demand after the wife-taking bachelor bungled his speech. The pig proved unhealthy and soon died, which further soured the relationship between Funo Loik and his affines.)

    In his speech, the wife-taking bachelor proclaims the inferiority of his lineage, the friendship he hopes will develop between the two groups, and his kinsmen's honesty. The desire to create a mutually profitable partnership is symbolized by the bridewealth, which in the speech is poetically called the "traveling bag" and "traveling sack." Even more humbly, the speaker describes the bridewealth as "modest" and "not good." This statement the wife-givers' acceptance speech contradicts. In his reply the wife-giving bachelor confirms the good quality of the gifts (lines 24–25). The bag and sack are mentioned because since they are woven from dried palm leaves it is possible for someone to look inside and inspect the quality of their contents. Since these contents cannot be disguised, the (honorable) motives of the wife-takers are visible: "No stone covers them," "no tree hides them." The idea of union occurs in both speeches, and on line 26 of the first speech the number three is used concisely to express this idea: "we two lineages have come together and made three." There are, of course, only two lineages, but the unity created by their coming together makes a sort of "third" in the native imagination. Now to the speeches.

The wife-taking bachelor says:

"Old women, old men   1
Brothers- and sisters-in-law—affines
Old women, old men
As inferiors we come from below
We arrive from the other world   5
We have brought you a traveling bag
We have fetched you a traveling sack
Its material is modest
Its workmanship is not good
Still, it reveals   10
It shows
You, our brothers- and sisters-in-law
Male affines
And female affines
As well as our mothers   15
All you might want to see
All you might want to hear
So we can know each other
So we can understand each other
Thus you, brothers- and sisters-in-law   20
Male affines
And female affines
As well as our mothers
Will have already guessed
Have surely already figured out   25
Why we two lineages have come together and made three

Hence our revelation
Without any hidden motives
No stone covers them
No tree hides them." 30

The wife-giving bachelor answers:

"Old women, old men 1
Brothers- and sisters-in-law—affines
Old women, old men
Today
Now 5
The bride
The groom
Bring we two lineages
Bring we two descent groups
Into a union 10
Into a union
We are now affines
We are now in-laws
You have brought us a traveling bag
You have fetched us a traveling sack 15
To reveal
To show
All we might want to see
All we might want to hear
So now we all know 20
We most definitely know
That this sack
That this bag
Is of *good* quality
We don't reject it 25
We don't refuse it
Even were it poor in quality
We wouldn't refuse it
We wouldn't refuse it
It's enough that our two lineages 30
In-law with in-law
Affine with affine
Are united
Are united

To carry the news of our agreement with our mouths   35
To carry the news with our voices
To make our mouths say nice things
To make our words sweet
The bridewealth
We exchanged for the bride   40
Whom we have now united with the groom
They are, as it were, at the end of a house beam
At the top of a tree
And are able to look down
By night as well as by day   45
On our two lineages, in-laws and in-laws
On our two lineages, affines and affines
Helping us in our secular affairs
Helping us in our sacred affairs
The bridewealth   50
With which to instill fertility into bride and groom
With which to blow life into their bodies
Making their bodies
Making their bodies
Healthy   55
Healthy
And able to produce offspring like betel
Capable of producing offspring like areca
Sprouting abundantly
Fertilizing abundantly   60
Not drying up like water
Nor dying like fire
Filling the rice field
Filling the rice terraces
Because they live in our princedom   65
Because they reside in our *u'e matan*
Multiplying themselves in our princedom
Multiplying themselves in our *u'e matan*."

The four bachelors then chew betel while their women serve meat, vegetables, and wine. The meal takes an hour, and as they depart the wife-taking bachelors remark:

"With potatoes we leave
Treading heavily we leave
We go naked and late."

Miguel Soares' wife weaving a *tais*, which is the formal dress worn for rituals and other important occasions.

They "leave with potatoes" because after giving their (prodigious!) bridewealth this humble tuber is all they have left. They "tread heavily" because they are downhearted at having had to surrender so much of their wealth. They "go naked" because their possessions have all gone toward making up the bridewealth. They "go late" because it has taken them so long to be relieved of their wealth. It *had* been so huge!

The wife-giver's speech overflows with images of union and fertility, which transcend sexual intercourse and affinal alliance. Lines 39–68 stress the creative function of these two types of union. They suggests that this gift, by making these two unions determines fertility. The *u'e*, as in previous speeches, joins with the idea of "multiplication"; and an association (again found in earlier speeches) is made between the fertility of the married couple and that of the rice-lands (lines 63–64). The earth is symbolically equivalent to the wife's womb, and the rice seed the husband's sperm. Hence the rice crops equal children. The theme of union-leading-to-creation, both at the sexual level and affinally, is clearly expressed in the ritual words assigned the priestess and bachelors. The third and most basic union, that of human beings and ancestral ghosts (secular and sacred), is not as explicit, though the priestess does pray to the ghosts, asking that sickness be kept at bay and requesting that the sexual and affinal unions be creative. Indeed, the villagers expressly claim that the union between humans and ghosts must be successful for the other two unions to succeed. When she addresses the couple the priestess represents both the ancestral ghosts and the old women and old men of the two lineages. Guardians of tradition and those humans nearest the next world, old people are regarded as being almost like (material) ghosts themselves. These senior persons do their best to make sure the younger members of the community, especially those about to be married, are aware of their lineage responsibilities. The ghosts provide spiritual sanction. These are tangibly manifested as infertility, sickness, and death. To avoid secular and sacred punishments bride and groom must obey traditional rules. In her second speech (lines 3–4) the priestess makes this clear when she remarks: "may our traditions and rules as well as the breath penetrate your bodies." Breath, life, rules, fertility, health, and *union-leading-to-creation* are part of the same dispensation.

After the ceremony the wife-takers return to their hamlets to continue gathering what bridewealth they still lack. A few weeks usually suffice to see this task completed, and then the wife-taking bachelors invite their wife-givers to attend the nuptial banquet in the hamlet of the groom's father. At this time, they also renew their invitation to the Caraubalo chief, João de Sá Viana.

Stage 4

The highlights of this final stage are the giving of the outstanding bridewealth and the meal that is given for the two lineages and their guests. Even though some wealthier descent groups would have the resources to deliver all the gifts as early as Stage 3, such a premature surrender is forbidden. In cases where all the gifts are ready Stage 4 occurs a few days after Stage 3.

Stage 4 is performed more casually than its predecessors. After the marriage gifts have been surrendered, the kin of both groups and members of both sexes eat together in a makeshift house. This rite of eating together—or *commensality*—symbolizes the integration of the two sexes, lineages, and ghosts and humans. The chief accompanying activity is story-telling. Because this is not an occasion for stressing divisions in society or the cosmos, storytellers are prohibited from reciting myths exclusively owned by either lineage. General narratives of origin (for instance, the myth of Rubi Rika, Lera Tiluk, and Cassa Sonek) and fabulous adventures, such as the story of Bui Lailua, are popular at weddings. So are animal fables, which contain a moral lesson.

The following tale, besides being amusing, teaches the value of cooperation. Although it particularizes the relationship between elder brother (a role enacted here by Shark) and younger brother (Monkey), all who listen to it appreciate that its lesson applies equally to relations between wife-givers and wife-takers and ghosts and humans: if cooperation is abandoned in favor of rivalry, at least one partner will suffer. The fact that it is Monkey who loses makes the story appealing at the pure narrative level, for in the many adventures which befall him in other stories, Monkey rarely fails to overcome his rival by trickery (Shark, Dog, and Crocodile are his usual stooges), and villagers delight at hearing how this smart little creature gets a taste of his own medicine.

Once upon a time big Shark lived in the sea and little Monkey lived on land. Shark was the elder brother; Monkey the younger. Both jointly owned a garden. They also shared the labor. Monkey did the work which required speed and agility, Shark the work that called for strength and toughness. Both needed each other.

One day Monkey lied to Shark, "Shark, if in good conscience I am to eat the food we have grown I must bring my wife and children to share it." Now Shark disliked this proposal. He informed his younger brother it would be fairer to split their garden into halves and each have his own half. But greedy Monkey proposed an alternative plan. "Better still, let's race for the whole garden, winner take all." Shark agreed, and Monkey thought the garden was as good as his. They arranged to compete next day.

Now Shark was not as bright as crafty Monkey, so that night he slipped into the sea to seek advice from his three smartest Shark friends. By the time dawn came they had worked out a ruse for tricking Monkey, and as the sun climbed over the palm trees the four Shark friends crawled into the garden. Each took up his position secretly along the track over which the race was to be run. The first Shark settled down at the starting line; the second farther along; the third still farther along the track; while Shark himself hid beside the finish line. No sooner were they settled in than along bounced Monkey in excellent spirits. "Well, Shark," he laughed, "are we all set to race?" Shark grunted, "Let's start!" Off they went. Monkey took off like a rocket, but Shark could only crawl slowly along. Shark just could not run! He was soon gasping for air. Monkey seemed to float over the ground. He seemed able to run forever. Shark could not keep up. He gasped and gasped as Monkey sprinted and sprinted. Shark could only gasp for air. When Monkey was halfway to the finish line he felt certain the garden was his. With a final burst of speed he stormed over the line. He had won!

But what he saw then made him howl with frustration. Ponderous Shark, dull-witted Shark, slow-moving Shark, was waiting for him! "Ha! Ha! Monkey!" chuckled Shark, "Halfway you seemed ahead, but I was really going faster all the time! Ah, yes! The garden's all mine now!" Wild though he was, Monkey could do nothing but trudge homeward crying, leaving the garden to Shark.

The corn ritual, described in chapter 3, demonstrated how symbolic action brings together (a) both sexes and (b) humans and ghosts. This chapter has described how in a second ritual these two unions interact with a third, the union between wife-takers and wife-givers. Both rituals are creative, and though one is agricultural and one is marital, both are inspired by the theme of *union-leading-to-creation*. But a second great theme inspires the collective thought and ritual system of the Mamulak Tetum: *Separation-leading-to-restoration*. Instead of heralding unity, this theme preaches division in the cosmos. How and why we shall now see.

Death: The cycle closes

7

The rigorous dualism of Tetum thought reinforces the common-sense observation that to think at all human beings must first divide up the undifferentiated world around them into clear-cut categories. Otherwise everything will be in a state of chaos. By themselves these categories have little meaning for it is the way in which they are inter-related that gives them this. The Caraubalo people follow other societies in manipulating the principles of opposition and complementarity to relate categories; and like human beings everywhere they exploit a third principle, that of analogy. Where they differ from most peoples is in the extent to which they apply these three principles, and the mythological and ritual use to which they put them. The most important of their categories are arranged according to these principles; and since the categories crystallize many of their most important ideas, we can say that the structure these principles help to form corresponds at an abstract level to the structure of the Tetum cosmos. It is 'an ordered system of ideas.' As an abstraction, this structure can be represented as a binary matrix (Figure 14).

The dyads contained in the matrix cohere into a set. Any single binary contrast can symbolize any other. We have already examined many ritual and literary contexts in which this property has been displayed. Other contrasts could be added to the list in Figure 14, but bulk is not the crucial matter. What matters is that over many generations the Tetum have found it convenient to compartmentalize experience in such a

(A)	(B)
human beings	ancestral ghosts
secular	sacred
secular world	sacred world
above	below
men	women
right	left
superior	inferior
wife-givers	wife-takers
aristocrats	commoners
secular authority	sacred authority
elder brother	younger brother

Figure 14   The Tetum Binary Matrix

way that it appears to consist of ideas that form contrasting pairs, and that many of these contrasting pairs are regarded as being in certain vital respects similar enough to stand for one another in specific situations. Tetum symbolism derives from such assumptions. This way of classifying is so pervasive that viewed from certain angles important sectors of life come together into a dual unity. A closer look at Figure 14 reveals that the first dyad refers to a religious contrast, the second to a metaphysical contrast, the third to a geographical contrast, the fourth to a spatial contrast, the fifth to a sexual contrast, the sixth to a lateral contrast, the seventh to a status contrast, the eighth to a kinship contrast, the ninth to a class contrast, the tenth to a governmental contrast, and the eleventh to another kinship contrast. These eleven contrasts belong to ten different spheres of experience, yet are brought together into a meaningful whole by the three principles of complementarity, opposition, and analogy to produce a unity which the French anthropologist Marcel Mauss

(1872–1950) would have called "a total social fact." Each contrast and the sphere to which it belongs shares its meaning with, and derives its meaning from, the other contrasts and their respective areas. To understand one contrast we must have knowledge of the others.

But life is not always orderly, and disorder is as much a feature of daily existence in Timor as it is anywhere. A fieldworker who concerns himself only with thought and behavior that fit into a conventional order allows much that is important to elude his understanding. I was therefore led to examine the ritual ways by which the Tetum handle the breakdown of order. In the cycle "order-disorder-order restored," the figures of witch and shaman and the ritual of death occupy central places.

As we have observed, health, political harmony, abundant crops, prosperous households, and the birth of children depend upon the orderly union of ancestral ghosts and their human kin, and upon the preservation of order in general. Ghosts and humans are two separate categories of being, yet they are regarded as complementary. Kept apart, they are nevertheless linked. If they are not joined in ritual, creation is impossible; if they are not kept distinct, the dual nature of Tetum thought will be eradicated. And since the totality of Tetum thought corresponds to the native cosmos, the loss of these distinctions will destroy the dual cosmos itself. Human affairs are, in daily reality, so variable and difficult to control that the Caraubalo system of categories is continually imperiled by the threat of chaos. Little effort is needed for an individual villager to turn cosmos into chaos. As I pointed out in chapter 2, a person who slights convention throws the order of his world into confusion. In effect, he erases the distinction between the categories listed in Column A and Column B of Figure 14. When the cosmos is set topsy turvy the residents of the sacred world have as much right to parade themselves in the secular world as human beings, and do not have to be evoked by ritual. Ghosts are able to appear in and around the hamlets, and (as in Bua Laran) can plague their kin. Since this interaction between ghosts and humans happens outside ritual, and comes about at the initiative of the ghosts, human beings have no control over this particular type of union, which becomes malignant instead of beneficial, destructive instead of creative. Quarrels between kin intensify, sickness and death befall the community, harvests fail.

Seeking a more abstract explanation, one who pursues a structural approach to the analysis of ideas and action would say that deviance symbolizes disorder. Since order is dual in character, the neat, well-insulated contrast between secular and sacred is turned into a new but confused category, which is both secular and sacred at the same time. But in the traditional binary matrix, no places exist for a category or pseudo-category which straddles both columns. A category must be clearly defined, and eligible for either Column A or Column B. If it cannot be fitted into one or other, it defies classification within the accepted universe of order. It is an anomaly, a mental monster which traditional thought cannot tame. If chaos is not to persist until it literally destroys the web of ideas underlying Tetum ideology, this monster must be tamed. Some anomalies are permanent landmarks of the ideological landscape. Shamans and witches are the most prominent. Impossible to eradicate, they are ever-present symbols of the chaos which constantly threatens to engulf humanity.

Invalids, corpses, dead souls, and the close kin of dead persons are temporary symbols of the chaos which follows human misbehavior, and a class of ritual exists to wipe out these anomalies by re-ordering their natures. Instead of *uniting* opposites, these rituals *separate* opposites which have become improperly united. Separation falls to the lot of such rituals as exorcism and the rites of death.

WITCHES

The hacking coughs and violent fevers, so much in evidence on the island, indicate that sickness exerts a tighter hold over Timorese life than among ourselves, and death (never an infrequent visitor to non-literate societies) makes its lurking presence continually felt. The Caraubalo folk take death into account in their daily affairs more frequently than Western urban dwellers do, and each day is looked upon as a struggle between the forces of life *(moris)* and death *(maté)*. This contrast they put to ritual use. Although many illnesses are ghostly punishments, the villagers believe that most come about as a result of the malevolence of creatures which are as much bona fide members of the secular world as they are of the sacred world. They are neither fully human nor yet fully spiritual. The Tetum call them "witches" *(buan)*.

Witches are persons credited with the talent to propel their souls through the air and penetrate the bodies of fellow villagers. A witch's soul, like that of an ordinary mortal, is normally invisible. It can change shape and size, so is capable of entering a victim's mouth, nose, or ear. Invasions occur at night while the victim is sleeping. At first invasions are infrequent, as the witch struggles to push the host soul out into the air. But if nocturnal visitations persist for a few nights in succession, some part of the victim's body will begin to ache. If a shaman is not promptly consulted, and if the witch takes a fancy to its host's body, the attacks become increasingly successful until the resident soul is pushed out. Weakness normally hinders its successful return. Should the soul be kept outside for about two weeks the body dies, whereupon the witch returns to its own body.

Most villages have a witch or two. How many, no one knows exactly for their identities are never established. As Evans-Pritchard in his *Witchcraft, Oracles, and Magic Among the Zande* (1937) remarks for the peoples of Central Africa, witchcraft is not a matter for public debate. Fear of witches was so widespread and intense among the Tetum I had difficulty getting even Agostinha, Rubi Loik, and André to talk about them. Leal Soares kept his lips tight.

From scraps of conversation I deduce that most witches are hermaphrodites. They are not hermaphrodites physiologically, but only in the way they regard themselves and are regarded by their neighbors. In these respects they resemble what one might call "ordinary" hermaphrodites. These are villagers who have no special link with the evil (or good) forces of the cosmos, but who if they are men prefer to behave like women and if they are women prefer to behave like men. Male hermaphrodites are called *fetok*. Their female counterparts are known as *manek*. The rest of the community tolerates them good-naturedly and does not force them to conform to the conventional sex roles. Mamulak had about six hermaphrodites. All were regarded as being potential witches (or shamans), but were not feared or especially respected on this account.

Because they slur the boundary between the sexes, hermaphrodites make admirable symbols of cosmic ambiguity. As witches (or shamans) they are both secular and sacred, a *permanent* and *absolute* condition which generates their power. In many cultures, individuals who bestride opposing categories, and things which defy pigeon-holing, are endowed with supra-normal powers. For example, the miracles Jesus Christ is said to have performed are consistent with his ambiguous status as a human being (secular) and as a god (sacred). With a foot in each camp, as it were, he could use both secular and sacred forces to a degree a being who was purely human or purely spirit could not.

In the routine of village life witches carry out their business like ordinary hermaphrodites until some misdemeanor disrupts the continuity of village life, whereupon a witch is prompt to pay the guilty person a nocturnal visit.

SHAMANS

Male as well as female, secular as well as sacred, the shaman is as ambiguous as a witch. But unlike the witch, who is an evil creature, a shaman is good. His native title is *matan do'ok*, "one who sees far." He ("she" or "it") is an individual who has a talent for diagnosing the causes of spirit possession or foretelling the future. He also acts as an exorcist and healer.

Mamulak's most celebrated shaman was Mateus, a twenty-five-year-old man from Bua Laran. His village had three shamans, but Mateus inspired the greatest confidence. He therefore charged the highest fees for his services: three piglets. After the advance payment has been made, the shaman escorts the invalid into the womb of his house. Here a sleeping mat lies spread out near a fire blazing in the hearth. Both sit on it. The shaman takes a betel leaf, a few pieces of areca and lime, places them in his mouth and chews. A couple of seconds later he spits a gob of the areca blood onto the floor. The spittle represents a mystic bridge between the two worlds. He must throw this bridge across to make connection with the spiritual power causing the trouble. This explains why areca blood is later daubed on the invalid's body and kept there. The shape of the gob of spittle and its shade of red tell the shaman what sort of spiritual attacker he is up against. If he decides an ancestral ghost is the invader, the shaman can only suggest what gift must be sacrificed by the victim to persuade the ghost to leave him in peace. But if the culprit is a witch, he can grapple with him mentally on the spot. Mateus used to say a careful scrutiny of the spittle can tell a skillful shaman, himself included, what his opponent's strengths and weaknesses are, thus improving his own chances of victory. Armed with this profile of his enemy, the shaman again chews betel. After a few minutes he extracts the reddish mass from his mouth and rubs it on the invalid's forehead and wherever pain is felt. Serving notice to humans and spirits alike of the contest taking place, the stains remain until the invalid is cured—or dies. The shaman stains the sick person three or four times daily. If the shaman's willpower proves stronger than that of the witch, he will sooner or later thrust the alien soul out. So the shaman sits night after night on the same mat as the victim, to protect him and prevent the evil soul from re-entering his body. When the witch realizes the hopelessness of its evil ambition, the shaman's nightly visits end and the sick person recovers. He returns home to offer a sacrifice which makes amends for whatever offense his shaman tells him caused the possession. Should the shaman prove weaker than the witch, however, the victim's health deteriorates until death claims his body. Sometimes a despairing invalid pays a second shaman to attempt a cure, hoping the new man knows something his colleague does not. But the result is seldom happier. Death, when it comes, symbolizes the cosmos in total disruption. It demonstrates the power of the ambiguous in Tetum thought, and threatens the deceased's lineage kin.

RITES OF PASSAGE

In 1909, before the development of modern fieldwork methods, the French scholar Van Gennep (1873–1957) pointed out that all rituals performed at the life-stages of birth, marriage, and death displayed a similar pattern. This was one of the most useful discoveries made in cultural anthropology. The pattern he discovered consists of three sub-rituals. He called these "rites of passage" because each enables an individual to move from one status in society to another. He explained that the opening sequence of any single rite of passage consisted of symbols of *severance* (such as circumcision, the removing of the foreskin from the penis of an adolescent male or baby); the next sequence consists of symbols of *segregation* (as in the Irish death wake) and the third sequence consists of symbols of *integration* (such as immersing a baby in baptismal water).

According to Van Gennep, when an individual is born, acquires a spouse, or dies, his status in the community and in the cosmos alters radically. For instance, when a bachelor marries, his role in society—what he is entitled to expect in the way of treatment from others, and what they expect from him—changes so drastically his passage from the state of bachelorhood to that of married man must be ceremonially marked, for all to see. Hence the public performance of what Van Gennep decided to call rites of passage. Three stages were necessary, he argued, because the changeover in status presented dangers for both the individual and for society. These dangers stemmed from the confusion occurring when a familiar individual exchanges an old role for a new one. A married man does not change physically in order to fit his new status; visibly and tangibly he remains the same. Thus the danger exists that his neighbors (more familiar with his old status than with his new status) may fail to take his added responsibility and authority seriously, and regard his new status as superficial as a change of clothing. This attitude would demean the status society grants married men, and would thus trivialize society itself. Ritual helps bring image, role, and individual together. But the ritual would still have to diminish this potential danger by first *severing* the initiate from his bachelorhood; hence the rites of severance. After the rites of severance, he is neither bachelor nor married man, an anomaly who does not fit neatly into any of the categories of his culture. His anomalous existence endangers the orderly character of his society's system of classification, and so is the most perilous of the three stages. Therefore, Van Gennep suggested, a person upon entering this stage is *segregated* from the rest of his community. His isolation may be little more than token, or it may be literal and extreme. Someone in this limbo-like predicament normally cannot appear at public gatherings or partake of the regular life of the community. This is the longest of the three stages, lasting in some rituals for over a year. After this stage, the rites of integration, in which the man is *integrated* into his new role, conclude the series. When the initiate emerges as a married man all traces of his previous status have been eradicated. He is fully fledged.

Making allowances for their necessary individual differences, these remarks apply equally to those transformations of status occurring at birth, marriage, and death. Not all societies use rites of passage when these life-stages occur. Neither do we always find that in every rite of passage each of the three stages will be equally well defined. But the underlying logic of performance, so brilliantly uncovered by Van Gennep, nevertheless holds up. The Caraubalo death ritual conforms exactly to his model.

DEATH

Death creates three anomalies in Tetum thought. First, the *corpse* is both secular and sacred. Although it is the vessel that held a former villager's soul, its lack of animation makes it different from what it used to be. Second, as a spirit the *dead soul* is sacred, yet flits about the hamlet where humans dwell. Third, sharing the corpse's status, its *surviving kin* are also regarded as anomalous.

To solve this classificatory problem, a rite of passage must be carried out. In Caraubalo this ritual involves rites of passage for three things: the corpse itself; the deceased's soul; and the dead person's lineage kin. Its intentions are to remove the corpse and dead soul from the secular world and fix them firmly in the sacred, and to sever the lineage kin from their tie with the sacred world and restore them to secular life.

Let us now return to the events of that May afternoon in 1967 and describe the ritual treatment meted out to seventy-year old Cai Tuli's corpse, dead soul, and hamlet kin after he had died following a brief illness on the fourteenth of the month.

The corpse

Rites of severance. In this initial stage a group known as the "people who give life" *(ema moris)* sever the ambiguous corpse from the secular community in which it once lived as a person.

Normal deaths take place in the rear compartment of the house, so what was once a womb for Cai Tuli now became a tomb. The ailing man breathed his last at 11 A. M., but four hours earlier his close lineage kin had sent out two bachelors to invite members of all the other lineages in the two villages to his funeral.

Affinal responsibilities between wife-givers and wife-takers focus on the death ritual. All the wife-giving and wife-taking lineages that had ever given or taken a wife from Cai Tuli's lineage were classed as "people who give life." Residents of other hamlets owned by Cai Tuli's lineage joined his own hamlet to form the group known as the "people of death" *(ema maté)*, because their kinship proximity to the deceased made them share his ambiguous status. To some degree they, too, were regarded as dead. Except for a short period on the fifth day of the ritual, they had passive roles to play. By restoring cosmic order, the "people who give life" make the union of opposites, hence creation and life, again possible. Their role is accordingly an active one.

Cai Tuli's hamlet was on the lineage territory of Maneiku (Mane Tolu clan), and as soon as he had been declared dead the first of the "people who give life," thrusting their way through the jungle grasses, burst into the hamlet in so timely a fashion I suspect they had been waiting outside for the news. Other "people who give life" joined them at intervals, and by the time the last few stragglers turned up the earliest arrivals had been hard at work for several hours. While the women prepared food and drink, their men hollowed out the soft trunk of a sago palm into a coffin, built the "death" house that was to temporarily retain the corpse, and made the open-sided, roofed building in which the final ceremonial meal was to be eaten. By the time these jobs had been completed, most of those who had been invited had added their labor. Cai Tuli's body was meanwhile washed, his hair cut, and his nails pared by other "people who give life." Then they dressed the corpse in its "clothing of death" and slipped it into the coffin. They next smashed a few of his personal belongings, including his bow and arrows; but spared his sacred pitcher and an assortment of other items, which would be destroyed in the *keta maté* ritual a year later. Actions of this kind symbolize the idea of "severance." After completing them the "people who give life" lifted up

Four *ema moris* split the trunk of a sago palm to make the lid of Cai Tuli's coffin. *Right:* Hollowing out a sago palm to make Cai Tuli's coffin. The trunks of palms are used because their pith is very soft.

the coffin and carried it into the back room of the death house, which they had built at one end of the village, where jungle (linked in the native imagination with the sacred) and village (associated with the secular) come together. These tasks took up most of the day, but the "people who give life" labored feverishly to get the corpse in its "betwixt and between" lodging before twilight, that transition period when witches begin to stir. To have a corpse on your hands then is asking for trouble, or rather double trouble, for the dead soul has already begun prowling around the houses.

Transporting Cai Tuli's body from his own house to the death house closed the first stage.

Rites of segregation. Cai Tuli's "betwixt and between" status provided the theme of this second stage. His corpse was no longer even partly secular, but neither was it yet sacred. So while the women of the "people of

Ema moris build a lean-to in which the funeral feast will be eaten after Cai Tuli's burial.

death" keened over it, it remained passively segregated from both worlds, at a place where they symbolically united, until the middle of the fifth day. The women's ceaseless wailing prevented everyone getting a proper night's rest during those nights. Upon returning home from a funeral, the first thing Maxine and I would do was get an undisturbed sleep. Larded with often insincere praise for the deceased Cai Tuli, the mourners' keening continued until the coffin was taken from the death house. As some mourners tired and left, others took their places and kept up the cries. Female keeners more distantly related, and less personally involved, competed to determine who could keen the loudest and longest. The "people who give life" kept away from the death house. Cooking, eating, gossiping, digging the grave, and putting together the stretcher upon which the coffin was to be borne to its final resting place kept them busy. This stage ended when the "people who give life," having decided to start the next stage arrived in front of the death house at noon on April 18.

Rites of integration. This stage incorporates the body in the world of the ancestral ghosts, giving it a sacred status in the cosmos.

When every guest had assembled, twelve bachelors carrying the stretcher stepped forward and dumped the coffin at the foot of the steps which rise to the front veranda of the death house. They were nervous, for at such moments the dead soul is certain to be hovering about ready to attack. Standing shoulder to shoulder in two equal groups on either side of the stretcher, they picked it up. With the stretcher grasped firmly in their hands the bachelors swayed gently from side to side, chanting a warning to the soul that if it returned to the body they would promptly expel it. Their swaying symbolized the act of expulsion. A soul which repossesses its body becomes a zombie, and the young men did not want to have to cope with that double anomaly—a creature both secular and sacred, both dead and alive. They had enough trouble keeping the soul at bay; at the meal ending the day's events they would tell tales of zombies and other grisly monsters, which would send shivers of terror down the spines of enthralled villagers.

The bachelors reinforced their warning gesture of swaying;

> "Poor orphan   1
> Poor fellow
> Your mother's no longer here
> Your father's no longer here
> Your mother's dead   5
> Your father's dead
> We are about to bury you
> In our local cemetery
> Come ancestral ghosts
> Come ancestors   10
> Walk with us
> Come near us
> And enter this hamlet!"

These words informed Cai Tuli's dead soul it was no longer a legitimate member of the hamlet. The speech implies that the soul lacks living kin (because of the real or false "death" of the mother), and so should not in any case want to resume residence. It also implies that the bachelors are about to place it in the ancestral world, which is now its proper home. Their invitation to the ghosts warns the dead soul that these beneficent spirits will be on hand to thwart any mischief it might be scheming.

Dressed as warriors about to set out on a head-hunting expedition, two married men had in the meantime taken up positions near the

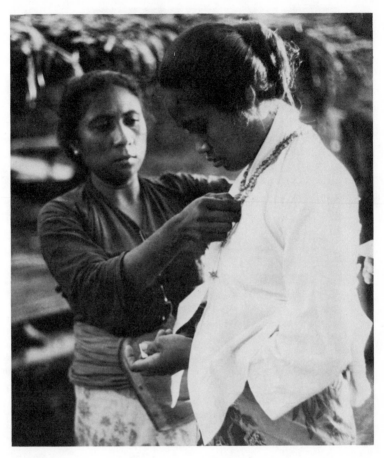

At Cai Tuli's funeral Agostinha helps Haré Lequik dress.

stretcher, while two female virgins, standing on mats, were being dressed in ritual clothing. The junior woman was Abo Nahak, and her companion was Haré Lequik. Both came from Mane Hat, and the latter had Agostinha as her dresser.

These virgins would lead the procession because the jungle is associated with ghosts and dead souls, and never having entered into carnal union with members of the secular sex they are thought to be less strongly attached to the secular world than married women. Behind them in the procession come the warriors, then the twelve bachelors carrying

Haré Lequik and Abo Nahak about to lead Cai Tuli's funeral *cortège* to the cemetery.

the coffin tied to the stretcher, and then, bringing up the rear, the rest of the community.

Their speech over, the bachelors mounted the steps, entered the house, tied the coffin to the stretcher, and carried it out. Then the "people of death" (except one) surged around the coffin. They placed their hands upon it. A minute later they retreated, leaving only Cai Tuli's widow, Namo Fahik, and a few intimate kin. Like the other "people of death," the widow was publicly asserting her desire that the corpse remain permanently in the hamlet with her. But the "people who give life" had other plans. Their responsibility was to install the body in the sacred world, and so even though Namo Fahik clung tearfully to the coffin the bachelors dragged it from her hands and started for one of the paths leading into the jungle.

Suddenly, the nerves of the bachelors—raw as uncoated wire from the heightening tension—were shattered by a spine-tingling shriek. They stopped dead in their tracks. For five days Cai Lequik, the thirty-year-old nephew of Cai Tuli, had been hiding away from the rest of the hamlet. Patiently, he had awaited his cue to enact the role of "lord of death." His great moment had at last come. Emerging dramatically from the depths of the house, he hurled himself down the steps at the coffin bearers, brandishing a massive sword in his clenched fist and bellowing at the bachelors to release the coffin. Terrified, the lads seemed about to drop their burden when the group of warriors began moving resolutely toward the fearsome apparition. Cai retreated abruptly into the house, leaving the bachelors free to complete their task. By the time they entered the jungle the entire population had joined them. Then, led by Haré Lequik and Abo Nahak, the procession meandered its way to the cemetery.

As at every funeral, the coffin was "attacked" seven times on its journey as the soul tried to pry off the lid and regain control over the corpse. Each time the coffin bearers mimed a fierce struggle with it until after the seventh tussle—just before they reached the cemetery—when the dead soul gave up. Their scuffling was particularly energetic this afternoon, for the mettlesome young men wanted to put on a rousing show, and to me they seemed to be upsetting the coffin's stability so much I offered a hand. . . .

Before lowering the coffin into the grave (a symbol of the sacred world's Mahuma "vagina"), the bachelors wrapped it in two palls of gorgeous coloring, "the clothes of death." These symbolized the larger, earthy womb of the sacred world in which the corpse is to remain forever entombed. The bachelors brought the third stage to an end by filling-in the vagina with soil. Then everyone walked back to the hamlet to eat the funeral meal and listen to horror stories.

"The people of death"

Before leaving to keen in the death house or in nearby houses (the stage of *segregation*), the "people of death" approached the "people who give life" to have their hair cut and their nails pared. For them, this was the rite of *severance*. Then followed the second stage. The third stage commenced when the "people of death" accompanied the coffin to the cemetery and ended with the feast which they ate with the "people who give life" after they had all returned to the village. This ritual of commensality *reintegrated* these temporary outcasts into village life, restoring them to the secular world. No longer were they the "people of death."

When everyone has eaten his fill, the congregation gathers around the storytellers and sits enrapt as tales of death chill their blood. The following is typical of the horror stories told at such gatherings. Leal Soares told it, and it was one of the most gruesome heard that night:

Two brothers lived together. A kinsman died. They decided to keen over his corpse. The younger brother was frightened; the elder was not. The coward sat far from the body. The brave brother sat very near. Having no fire the elder ordered his younger brother to go out for a firebrand. After the coward had left, the brave brother grabbed the corpse and made it a pillow for his head. With his head on the cold pillow he dropped off to sleep.

The younger brother had meanwhile met a boy carrying a firebrand. He seized it. Returning home his first words were, "Oh! I'm scared of the corpse!" His elder brother replied, "O.K! Fetch it here!" The coward said, "Can't. Too frightened!" The brave brother stalked over to him, snatched the firebrand, and clambered up the stairs into the "tomb" ["womb"] of the house where the corpse lay. But just as he was staring into the dead face

he suddenly, to his horror, saw the corpse revive! The coward screamed in terror, but his elder brother quickly regained his nerve. The corpse then began to get up! Jumping down the stairs, the coward rushed out of the hamlet and ran for a hill. He certainly was a coward! His brother ran from the house more slowly. He was a bad sprinter, and the corpse began catching up with him. The brave brother ran to the tall tree in which the coward was hiding, and started climbing it. It was tough work!

The corpse reached the foot of the tree and shouted up, "Your gossiping revived me. I can now walk. Come down!" "Oh!" replied the coward, "I'm too frightened to come down." "You can't stay up there forever," mocked the corpse. "Your brother should have made sure my soul was safely in the sacred world before fooling around with me." Then, taking hold of the tree it shook the branches until the coward was thrown down. The corpse grabbed him. Then it shook the tree a second time, and down fell the elder brother. And so the two brothers died.

Stories of this kind filled the air until night gave way to dawn. By then all the guests had left. For Cai Tuli's corpse and the "people of death" the ritual was over.

Left: In this mortar corn and rice are pounded at funerals, births and marriages. The two poles attached to the mortar enable men to carry it from one place in a hamlet to a site more convenient for the cooks. In the background is the table upon which the funeral meal will be later eaten.

Agostinha (left foreground) and other women pound rice at a funeral.

The dead soul

Cai Tuli's dead soul was less easily reckoned with than was his body. For it, the rites of severance extended from the departure of the living soul from the body (physical death), through the shaking of the stretcher, to the seventh tussle. This was the symbolic final separation of body and soul. Villagers believe that between the time of death and the final struggle the soul flits around the hamlet seeking an opportunity to re-enter the body. Unlike the corpse and its surviving kin, a dead soul is invisible. Humans can never be quite certain it has negotiated a particular stage of the ritual and become an established member of the sacred world. This uncertainty explains why each of the three stages for the soul is much longer than for the corpse and kin, and why multiple severances are performed. Villagers take no chances with an unseen monster!

Segregation lasts exactly one year from the day the coffin is interred. During this period Cai Tuli's soul, though no longer a legitimate inhabitant of the secular world, was not yet classed as an integrated member of the ancestral ghosts' world. Its ambiguous status enabled it to pass back and forth from one domain to the other, rejected by humans yet not acknowledged as a true sacred being by the ancestral ghosts. For the deceased's kin these twelve months were filled with anxiety. Only the shamans knew how to locate the elusive soul, which all the while enjoyed causing sickness in its old hamlet. Mateus earned many piglets that year.

The rites of integration (the *keta maté*) lasted only part of an afternoon. They were followed by a festival that persisted into the early hours of the next morning. Once more the "people of death" and the "people who give life" assembled in Cai Tuli's hamlet. Again the "people who give life" set about ridding the community of an unwelcome anomaly. Their symbolic acts, intended to emphasize final severance, consisted of tearing up, smashing, and mutilating those of Cai Tuli's possessions (his sacred pitcher, sleeping mat, and clothing) which they had withheld from the earlier destruction. The debris they tossed into the jungle, where it would rot in the rain and sun until winds swept it from the sight of human beings. In this way, these symbols of Cai Tuli's soul were integrated into the sacred womb, symbolized here by the jungle wilderness. At last his soul lay at rest.

In her intriguing book *Purity and Danger*, Professor Mary Douglas argues (1966:143): "Any given system of classification must give rise to anomalies, and any given culture must confront events which seem to defy its assumptions. It cannot ignore the anomalies which its scheme produces, except at the risk of forfeiting confidence. That is why, I suggest, we find in any culture worthy of the name various provisions for dealing with ambiguous or anomalous events." Anomalies challenge the system of categorical order upon which culture is based, and among the Caraubalo Tetum the results of unions unsanctioned by society are so confusing that two of their physical manifestations are sickness and death. Creation depends upon opposites coming together in a regulated manner, and if the fundamental contrasts, secular and sacred, have been replaced by a single pseudo-category which is both secular and sacred at the same time, creation is impossible. To restore traditional order and make creation (upon which the continuance of life depends) again possible the separation rituals of exorcism and of death are performed. By separating what has been improperly united they enact the second great theme of Tetum collective thought: separation-leading-to-restoration.

Many societies believe ghosts and other spirits exist in a sacred world they class as opposite to their own secular world. Success in human endeavor may depend upon these sacred beings, who impose sanctions for moral and social behavior. If this belief is prominent in a society, and if that society's commitment to cosmic order is sufficiently entrenched in the minds of its members, the relationship between humans and ghosts may well figure prominently in many spheres of life. When we examine Tetum culture, taking the ritual relationship between ancestral ghosts and their human kin as our starting point, such different spheres as rituals, religious beliefs, kinship practices, oral literature, ecology, and architecture together blend into a single, expansive field of study.

Glossary of Tetum words

Ahi matan   Village; clan; hearth.
Ai suak   Digging stick, or dibble.
Alin   Younger sibling.
Ali-maun   Agnates of a clan.
Buan   Witch.
Cain   Stalk; stem; descent group; umbilical cord.
Dato ua'in   One of the two traditional leaders of Caraubalo princedom; the other being the *macair fukun*. The office of *dato ua'in* is owned by the Ina Aman clan in the village of Mamulak.
Ema maté   The lineage agnates of a dead person, the "people of death."
Ema moris   The "people who give life," who perform vital ritual functions when a person in Mamulak or Mane Hat dies.
Feto   Female, woman, feminine.
Feto fuan, mane fuan   Lineage.
Fetok   A man who chooses to behave like a woman; a male social hermaphrodite.
Folin   Bridewealth.
Fona   Opening; door; vagina.
Foti feto   An uncommon form of commencement for a *hafoli* marriage, in which the bride elopes with her lover.
Habani   The second most important type of marriage in Caraubalo. It involves a regime of matrilineal descent and uxorilocal residence, and no bridewealth.

Hafoli   The most important type of marriage in Caraubalo. It involves a regime of patrilineal descent and patrilocal residence, and bridewealth.

Halo batar moris   The corn-planting ritual.

Hena lolon   The sacred cloth, "the womb made of cloth"; a cloth of considerable symbolic value in Tetum ritual. Also called the *hena mean tahan ida*.

Hena meân tahan ida   The sacred cloth; a cloth of considerable symbolic value in Tetum ritual. Also called the *hena lolon*, "the womb made of cloth."

Hussu feto   The most common form of commencement for a *hafoli* marriage.

Keta maté   The final rite of the death ritual.

Klamar   Soul. That inside a living body is called the *klamar moris;* that which death has freed from the body is called the *klamar mate.*

Klamar maté   The soul of a dead person; a dead soul.

Klamar moris   The soul of a living person.

Lolon   Womb.

Lulik   Sacred; prohibited. In Tetum thought and ritual this term is opposed to *sa'un.*

Macair fukun   One of the two traditional leaders of Caraubalo princedom; the other being the *dato ua'in.* The office of *macair fukin* is owned by the Mane Tolu clan in the village of Mane Hat.

Mane   Male, man, masculine.

Manek   A woman who chooses to behave like a man; a female social hermaphrodite.

Matan   Eye; center; source.

Maté   To die; death; dead. Its complementary opposite is *moris.*

Maté bian   Ancestral ghost.

Maun   Elder brother.

Moris   To live; life; to be living. Its complementary opposite is *mate.*

Modok   "The green vegetables," the five *patacas* and a sacred cloth known as the *hena meân tahan ida*, which forms one of the two parts of the symbolic bridewealth (the *na'an tolu*). The other part is called the *na'an.*

Na'an   "The meat," of a buffalo, a horse, a pig, and fifty *patacas*, which forms one of the two parts of the symbolic bridewealth (the *na'an tolu*). The other part is called the *modok.*

Na'an tolu   That part of the bridewealth which has symbolic significance; the symbolic bridewealth.

Oda matan   The steps to the source of life, that is, to the interior of the house.

Pataca   An old Mexican coin imported centuries ago into Timor.

Rai   The earth; kingdom; the dwelling place of human beings. This term is opposed in Tetum thought and ritual to *rai laran.*

Rai laran   The womb of the earth; the Earth Mother; the dwelling place for ghosts and other spirits; the place where human beings originated and where their bodies and souls return at death. This region is opposed in Tetum thought and ritual to *rai.*

Rai na'in   Aristocratic population of Caraubalo princedom; demon.

Ri kakuluk   The ritual pillar near the back of the house. Around it about four feet from the floor is the ritual shelf which contains ritual paraphernalia.

Sai rai   "To leave the earth"; the mythological emergence of the first human beings (the earliest inhabitants of Caraubalo) from the earth; the birth ritual, which re-enacts this event.

Sai tan feto   The second most common form of commencement for a *hafoli* marriage. It occurs when a girl becomes pregnant.

Sa'un   Secular; profane; not prohibited. In Tetum thought and ritual this term is opposed to *lulik*.

Tuna   Eel. Also name of a Mamulak clan.

U'e   Liquid; water; source; a symbolic link between humans and ghosts.

U'e lolo oan   The sacred water pitcher which is used in important rituals, such as birth and death.

U'e matan   Well; spring. Source of life for inhabitants of Caraubalo princedom, which is a large vent (the "Mahuma vagina") in earth's surface. Used figuratively in parallel contexts.

Uma   House.

Uma lolon   The "womb" of the house, the rear room. Here the house rituals are performed.

List of anthropological terms

Ancestral ghosts   Souls of ancestors of a descent group.

Acculturation   The process whereby a culture exchanges its values and institutions for those of an alien culture.

Affine   A relative by marriage.

Agnate   A person related to another by patrilineal descent.

Alliance group   That descent group whose members contribute toward, or who receive upon distribution, the bridewealth. It may be a clan or lineage; among the Tetum it is the lineage.

Analogical association   A logical principle which relates one thing to another by evoking some resemblance; for example, man is to woman as right is to left as secular is to sacred.

Apical ancestor   The ultimate ancestor from whom descent is traced; so-called because this individual is at the "apex" of the triangle of descendents.

Bridewealth   Gifts given by the wife-taking alliance group to the wife-giving alliance group.

Classificatory thought   The ideas members of a community hold collectively and the ways in which they are ordered.

Commensality   Eating together.

Complementary opposition   A binary contrast or dyad in which each term of the contrast is related to the other by being both its opposite and its complement; for example, man and woman, right and left, secular and sacred.

Endogamy   A rule requiring marriage to take place inside a specified social class, group, or category.

Exogamy   A rule requiring marriage to take place outside a specified descent group or range of kin.

Expressive ritual   A ritual whose chief function is to express certain symbolic themes or ideas rather than to bring about any changes in the world; for example, the Tetum ritual of birth commemorates the Caraubalo myth of origin.

Instrumental ritual   A ritual whose chief function is to bring about a change in the world rather than merely express symbolic themes or ideas; for example, the Tetum death ritual changes the cosmic statuses of corpse, kin, and dead soul.

Kin   Clansfolk. In a patrilineal system this term is synonymous with "agnate."

Patrilocal residence   Post-marital residence of a married couple with the husband's agnates.

Polygyny   Marriage of man to two or more women. If the women are sisters, this variation is called "sororal polygyny."

Ritual reversal   A situation in which roles, statuses, or symbolic associations are opposite to what they normally are; for example, a woman becomes superior to a man.

Sanctions   A penalty for disobedience or a reward for obedience.

Shaman   A religious figure, frequently described as an "inspired priest," whose authority is derived not from holding an inherited office, but from a talent for making contact with spirits—often while in a trance.

Social structure   This term has some very different meanings, one of which denotes a pattern in the institutions and values of a society which an observer finds useful to assume.

Symbolic classification   The ways in which the categories of a society are ordered.

Uxorilocal residence   Residence of a married couple with the wife's kin.

Recommended readings

TOPICAL WORKS

1. The best introduction to kinship is Robin Fox's *Kinship and Marriage*, published by Penguin Books (London, 1967), which clearly and in lively prose presents the fundamentals of kinship and marriage for readers unfamiliar with the anthropological approach.

2. David Maybury-Lewis's *The Savage and the Innocent*, published by Beacon Press (Boston, 1965), is the most candid account by a contemporary fieldworker of his trials, tribulations, and eventual triumph.

3. *Reader in Comparative Religion: An Anthropological Approach*, edited by William A. Lessa and Evon Z. Vogt, and published by Harper & Row (New York, 1958), is an indispensable collection of essays and extracts on myth, ritual, symbolism, and other aspects of religion by specialists in this topic.

REGIONAL WORKS

1. Marie Jeanne Adams has written several excellent analyses of eastern Sumbanese culture, but her most comprehensive work on these close relatives of the Tetum is *System and Meaning in East Sumba Textile Design: A Study in Traditional Indonesian Art*, Number 16 of the Yale University Southeast Asia Studies, Cultural Reports (New Haven, 1969). The three logical principles so frequently used by the Tetum recur in many areas of Sumbanese symbolism.

2. The outstanding modern structural analysis of any Indonesian society is the extraordinarily detailed *Kédang: A Study of the Collective Thought of an Eastern Indonesian People*, by Robert Barnes, published by Clarendon Press (Oxford, 1974). This is indispensable reading for anyone interested in the structural interpretation of Indonesian fieldwork data.

133

Bibliography

Beidelman, T. O., ed. *The Translation of Culture*. London: Tavistock Publications, 1971.

Cunningham, Clark. "Order in the Atoni House," *Bijdragen tot de Taal-Land—en Volkenkunde* 120 (1964):34–68.

Douglas, Mary. *Purity and Danger: An Analysis of Concepts of Pollution*. New York: Praeger, 1966.

Duarte, Jorge. "Barlaque," *Seara* 2 (n.s.) (1964):92–119.

Durkheim, Émile. *The Elementary Forms of the Religious Life*. Translated from the French by Joseph Ward Swain. New York: The Free Press, 1965.

Evans-Pritchard, E. E. *Witchcraft, Oracles, and Magic among the Zande*. Oxford: Clarendon Press, 1937.

Frazer, James. *The Golden Bough* (abr. ed.). London, 1922.

Hertz, Robert. "The Pre-eminence of the Right Hand: A Study in Religious Polarity," in *Right and Left: Essays on Dual Symbolic Classification*, Edited and with an Introduction by Rodney Needham. Foreword by E. E. Evans-Pritchard. Chicago and London: University of Chicago Press, 1974.

Keesing, Roger M. *Kin Groups and Social Structure*. New York: Holt, Rinehart, & Winston, 1975.

Leach, Edmund. "A Discussion on Ritualization of Behaviour in Animals and Man," *Philosophical Transactions of the Royal Society of London*, Series B, No. 772, Vol. 251 (1966).

Sá, Artur Basilio de. *Textos em Teto Literatura Oral Timorense*, Vol. 1. Lisbon: Junta de Investigações do Ultramar, 1961.

Schulte Nordholt, H. G. *The Political System of the Atoni of Timor.* Translated from the Dutch by M. J. L. van Yperen. The Hague: Martinus Nijhoff, 1971.

Turner, Victor. *The Forest of Symbols.* Ithaca: Cornell University Press, 1967.

Tylor, Edward B. *Primitive Culture,* Vol. I (2d. ed.). London: John Murray, 1873.

Van Gennep, Arnold. *The Rites of Passage.* Translated from the French by Monika B. Vizedom and Gabrielle L. Caffee. Chicago: University of Chicago Press, 1960.

Index

Page references to photographs are printed in *italic* type.

Property: passage of, 70, 71; types of,
72-73
Punishment: by ancestral ghosts, 27, 29,
82, 104, 109, 110, 125; for anti-clan
behavior, 69, 70, 82
Purity and Danger, 124

Radcliffe-Brown, A.R., 17
Religion: as criterion of acculturation,
10, 11; Durkheim's definition of, 20
Research methods and conditions, 8-18
Rice cultivation, 42, 50, 52, 53, 54-55
Right hand: associated with men, 23, 44,
93; associated with secular world, 44,
93
Rika, Rubi (ancestral ghost), 22, 23, 24,
31, 32, 33, 37, 78, 81, 105
Rites of passage, 113-25. *See also* Death
ritual
Ritual: classification of, 29; definition of,
29; and myth, 36; pattern of three
subrituals in, 113; unifying nature of,
1-2. *See also* Birth ritual; Corn ritual;
Death ritual; Marriage ritual; Sacred
rituals
Ritual reversal, 32, 85
Rui de Brito, 4

Sá, Father, 80
Sacred and secular, basic contrast
between, 20, 119, 125
Sacred rituals, 29. *See also* Ritual
Sacred world, 20, 23-29, 30, 80, 93, 125;
symbols of, 23, 31-34 *passim,* 44, 65,
85
St. Domingo's tree, in birth ritual, 33, 34
Salem, Massachusetts, witchcraft in, 28
Sandalwood, 4
Sá Viana, João da, 52, 53, 97, 104
Schulte Nordholt, H.G., 8
Seasonal cycle, 40-51
Secular and sacred, basic contrast
between, 20
Secular rituals, 29
Secular world, 20, 23, 29, 80, 93, 125;

symbols of, 23, 32, 44, 85
Segregation, rites of, 113, 114, 116-17,
121
Separation, rituals of, 30, 106, 110, 125;
in birth ritual, 30; in marriage ritual,
92
Servião empire, 4
Severance, rites of, 113, 115-16, 121,
124
Shamans, 34, 80, 109, 110, 111, 112-13,
124
Sickness, 80; caused by witch, 110-11;
disorder symbolized by, 24-25, 27,
28, 30, 109, 110, 124, 125; as ghostly
punishment, 27, 28, 110; treated by
shaman, 111-12
Siri Lari (village), 22, 51-52, 54, 55
Soares, Agostinha, 21-22, 38, 79, 111,
119, *119, 123;* stories told by, 22, 65-
66, 78
Soares, Ana, 47
Soares, Leal, 1, 19, 27, 111; story told
by, 122-23
Soares, Miguel, 7; wife of, *103*
Social anthropology, 17
Social organization of villages, 73, 75,
76, 79
"Social structure," subjective nature of,
17
Sociology vs. cultural anthropology, 14
Sonek, Cassa (ancestral ghost), 22, 23,
24, 31, 32, 33, 37, 81, 105
Soul, 24-26; definition of, 25;
immortality of, 24; of witch, 110-11,
112. *See also* Dead souls
Southeast Asia, mainland, 39
Spinsters, 86
Spirits, 125; anxiety inspired by, 45; fear
inspired by, 27-29; superiority in
sacred situations, 21, 45. *See also*
Demons; Nature spirits; Witches
Stones: in birth ritual, 21, 23, 33-34, 65,
66; in corn ritual, 42, 43
Storytelling: at birth ritual, 36; at death
ritual, 118, 122-23; at marriage ritual, 105

142